COMMENTARY ON THE SUNDAY LECTIONARY

Vol. 1. First Sunday of Advent
to Pentecost Sunday

YEAR TWO (1970)

PETER COUGHLAN
and
PETER PURDUE

GEOFFREY CHAPMAN
LONDON DUBLIN MELBOURNE 1969

Geoffrey Chapman Ltd
18 High Street, Wimbledon, London SW19

Geoffrey Chapman (Ireland) Ltd
5–7 Main Street, Blackrock, County Dublin

Geoffrey Chapman Pty Ltd
346 St Kilda Road, Melbourne, Vic 3004, Australia

Nihil obstat : John M. T. Barton STD, LSS, Censor
Imprimatur : + Patrick Casey VG
Westminster, 10.10.69

The Nihil obstat and Imprimatur are a declaration that a book or pamphlet
is considered to be free from doctrinal or moral error. It is not implied
that those who have granted the Nihil obstat and Imprimatur agree with
the contents, opinions, or statements expressed.

This book is set in 11 on 12pt. Intertype Baskerville

Made and printed in Great Britain by
A. Wheaton & Co., Exeter

Contents

Introduction : The New Lectionary   1

Introductions to Books Frequently Used in the Lectionary
1. The Book of Isaiah   9
2. The Book of Psalms   12
3. The Gospel According to St Mark   14
4. The Gospel According to St John   18
5. The Acts of the Apostles   22
6. The First Letter to the Corinthians   25
7. The Letter of St Paul to the Ephesians   27
8. The First Epistle of St John   30

The Christmas Cycle (1 Advent to Baptism of our Lord)

The Season of Advent   32

The Season of Christmas   42

The Yearly Cycle (Sundays 2—5 of the Year)   62

The Paschal Cycle (Ash Wednesday—Pentecost)
Lent   72

The Easter Triduum   88

Eastertide to Pentecost   100

Index of Sunday readings, by the day   120

Index of scriptural references   123

Introduction:
The New Lectionary

Condensed liturgy and condensed scripture are not figments of the imagination. It could be claimed that scholarly progress is outstripping the possibility of popularizing its findings. Yet the non-expert has a right to expect information and explanation that is brief and to the point.

We have a new Order of the Mass on our hands; this time not a mere rubrical juggling, but a new shape to the Roman liturgy, the first for centuries. But even this new Order is not as 'new' as the revision of the scripture readings at Mass. Not only have the readings themselves been altered for the most part, but even the system in which they are read.

This book has two jobs to do. It has to *explain* the new system of readings, especially to clarify the content of the readings themselves. It has also to *guide* the preacher and teacher in the ways of explaining the new readings to others. Brevity, we believe, is of the essence when users are busy people. We are concerned with the Sunday and Principal Feast Day Masses; and, in this first volume, from the First Sunday of Advent until Pentecost Sunday of Year Two. Two pages are devoted to each Mass. But supplementary information is given (i) about individual books of the Bible that are more prominent in the Lectionary, and (ii) about the major themes of the liturgical seasons.

How the new Lectionary is built up

Alternative Weekday Readings have been used in many churches for a number of years. So the idea of a cycle of readings will not be new.

1

The Liturgy Constitution of the Second Vatican Council programmed the reform of the Mass, and among these reforms was to be the revision of the Mass readings :

The treasures of the Bible are to be opened up more lavishly, so that richer fare may be provided for the faithful at the table of God's Word. In this way a more representative portion of the holy scriptures will be read to the people over a set cycle of years.[1]

For the past five years work has been going on to prepare the new Lectionary. The thoroughness of the work was quite remarkable : historical studies into previous lectionaries of all liturgical rites, including the readings of other Christian bodies; advice from biblical scholars about what should be included; consultation with parish priests and others engaged in pastoral work.

Though the new Lectionary has a structure very similar to the old one : a Proper of the Season, Sunday and Weekday; a Proper and Common of the Saints; Ritual and Votive Masses; it is better to talk separately about
(i)   the Sunday Lectionary,
(ii) the Weekday one, and
(iii) Masses for saints' feasts, whether Proper or Common, Ritual Masses and Votive Masses.
Only the Lectionary for Sundays and Principal Feasts need concern us here, save to mention that the cycle of Sunday readings (over three years) and the cycle of Weekday readings (over two years) are entirely independent.

The Sunday Lectionary—a three year cycle

Besides being the most important part of the new system of readings, the Sunday Lectionary has also the most variety, in order that people may hear a 'more representative portion of the holy scriptures' on the days they are obliged to attend Mass.

There is a three year cycle of Sunday readings. It is interesting to note that some scholars think the synagogue services in the time of our Lord had a cycle of three years for its readings. This

[1] *Sacrosanctum Concilium*, n. 51. Translation, W. M. Abbott and J. Gallagher, *The Documents of Vatican II*, Geoffrey Chapman 1966, p. 155.

cycle may have influenced the use of Old Testament quotations in the Gospels and even the structure of the Gospels themselves.

The use of a three year cycle allows the use of one Gospel per year : Matthew is read in Year One, Mark in Year Two, Luke in Year Three. St John's Gospel is read every year in the Lent–Paschaltide season.

How do we know which year of the cycle we are in? To avoid confusion a simple formula was devised. If the year number is divisible by three, that year is Year Three. A year begins on 1 January, but throws its number back onto the previous First Sunday of Advent. So 1970 is Year Two, because 1971, being a year divisible by three, is Year Three. Year Two begins on 30 November 1969 and ends 28 November 1970. The next Year Two will be 1973.

Three Readings

Each Mass on Sundays and the Principal Feasts will have three readings. The First is always taken from the Old Testament, except in Paschaltide when the Acts of the Apostles is used in place of Old Testament passages. The Second Reading is taken from the Letters of the New Testament or the Apocalypse. The Third is always a passage from one of the Gospels.

It is very strongly recommended that all three readings should be used. But a choice is permitted between the First and Second.

The three readings are intended to be about the same length as the two readings of the previous Missal. But there is another criterion of length : the ability of the passage to hold the attention of the congregation. A narrative reading can hold the attention more easily and so can afford to be longer than a doctrinal passage. Readings from St Paul, for example, are much shorter because of the conciseness of the thought and language.

The cure of the blind man in John, chapter 9 (read on the Fourth Sunday of Lent, Year One) gives a good example of the way the Lectionary allows a lengthier passage to be read when it is important to have the whole story. However, pastoral circumstances can make long readings very difficult. So a shorter version of long passages is given, with the hope that any anomalies will be ironed out in the homily.

Harmonization and semi-continuity

We may justly criticize the present Roman missal for not having a unity of theme in many of its Mass readings. A single theme would help the people to understand the texts better and give the preacher opportunity to unify his homily. This is going to be even more important when there are three readings.

The *harmonization* principle is 'One Mass One Theme' in all three scripture readings. The pastoral and catechetical advantages of this principle are obviously quite considerable. The new Lectionary has in fact adopted the 'One Mass One Theme' idea for the major Sundays and Feasts. The scriptures will thus illustrate the mystery being celebrated. We can expect, then, more attention to the harmonization of the readings in Advent and Christmas Masses, and in the Lent and Paschaltide periods. But even here there is, in Year Two for example, a predominance of Mark wherever possible, and the semi-continuous reading of John's First Epistle during Paschaltide.

Following ancient liturgical tradition and to avoid over-systematizing the Christian message, another principle for the choice of texts is used, that of *semi-continuity* : a series of passages from one book is read over several consecutive Sundays. Bearing in mind that the Word of God comes to us not in separate passages but in whole books, it is paramount that the liturgy should allow the more or less continuous reading of particular books so that the mind of the inspired author can be explained and his argument followed through.

The word 'semi-continuity' is used because there is too much material for the 'continuous' reading of all the Gospels in three years, and it was felt undesirable to read certain difficult passages or those of less importance. Even whole chapters are omitted from the Epistles for similar reasons. A four year cycle would be needed to read all the New Testament, but then there would be a considerable repetition of Gospel passages. So a three year cycle was decided upon and the necessary 'cutting' carried out.

Semi-continuity in Sunday readings is found for the most part on Sundays throughout the Year, the Sundays after the Epiphany and after Pentecost. It is employed only in the reading of New Testament books. In 1970, the predominant Gospel is the Gospel according to Mark. Mark is shorter than the other three, so five readings are inserted from John chapter 6, beginning at the end of July.

With regard to the Epistles, First John is read during Paschaltide, First Corinthians 6–11, Second Corinthians, Ephesians, James and Hebrews 2–10 are read on Sundays throughout the Year. First Corinthians is easily divided between all three years of the Sunday cycle because of the variety of content. But Hebrews was felt to be too difficult for the people to hear over more than ten Sundays, so it was divided between Years Two and Three.

Age-old traditions associating certain books with particular liturgical seasons have been retained. Thus there is a mixture of harmonization and semi-continuity in the reading of the Acts of the Apostles in Paschaltide to replace the Old Testament in the First Reading. First Peter, a baptismal Epistle; First John showing our status as children of God; and the Apocalypse, the prophecy of Christian hope, are considered paschal books and are read semi-continuously after Easter in Years One, Two and Three respectively. Isaiah is traditional for Advent, Jeremiah for Holy Week. And the spiritual depth of John's Gospel makes it the paschal Gospel *par excellence*. Not having a special year of its own, the Fourth Gospel is the predominant Gospel from mid-Lent until Pentecost.

It was not considered desirable to read Old Testament books semi-continuously. Rather, the Old Testament reading is meant to harmonize with the Gospel reading. Many Gospel passages quote or allude to the Old Testament, in which case the appropriate Old Testament text is read. The intention is to show the continuity of God's plan of salvation from the Old Testament to the Gospel. The Second Reading is then more concerned with Christian living.

On the more solemn Sundays and Feasts there is harmonization of all three readings, but on Sundays throughout the Year, harmonization of the Second Reading and the Gospel has been dropped. The preacher will need to beware of making unity out of diversity. Perhaps a solution of these occasions would be to give a *short* introduction to each reading and then dedicate the homily to just one of them.

The Responsorial Psalm

After the First Reading, the Lectionary indicates a Responsorial Psalm and Response. This Psalm should not be treated as an extra to the liturgy. It is an essential part of the celebration. Though especially related to the First Reading, to see it as the response to the Old Testament reading would be to restrict its real function. It serves as the official response of the faithful to the Word of God proclaimed to them in all the readings.

A particular psalm is chosen if the First or Second Reading quotes a psalm, or has similar language and content to one of the psalms. Similarly if the Gospel quotes a psalm, this psalm is used in the Response as an anticipation of the Gospel.

Liturgical tradition has associated certain psalms with major seasons of the year; with Christmas, the royal psalms 95, 96 and 97; in Lent, 25, 50, 90 and 129; in Holy Week, Psalm 21. These traditional Responsorial Psalms remain as the Church's chosen expressions of her mind in her most important liturgical seasons.

Very often it is the Response that is the link between the readings and the choice of the psalm. The Response is intended to be sung (or said) by the people, while the cantor or choir sing the verses of the Psalm.

In spite of the importance of the Response in the Responsorial Psalm, the Lectionary does envisage pastoral difficulties in learning a new one each week. So a list of Responses is provided for use over several weeks, during Lent or Paschaltide, for example. To make matters easier still, the already published Simple Gradual[1] gives common Responsorial Psalms which can replace the ones set for particular Masses over the weeks of a particular liturgical season.

The Alleluia

The Alleluia versicle has an entirely different origin from the Responsorial Psalm. Its purpose is to welcome Christ coming in the Gospel about to be read, with

---

[1] *The Simple Gradual for Sundays and Holydays*, ed. J. R. Ainslie, Full Music Edition for Choir and Cantor; Melody Edition for Congregation, Geoffrey Chapman 1969.

(i) an acclamation of praise, normally 'Praise the Lord' (Alleluia), or in Lent another type of acclamation such as 'Praise and glory to you, Lord Jesus', and

(ii) a versicle taken from the Gospel that follows or a phrase which sums up the theme of the Mass as a whole.

The Alleluia versicle may be omitted if it is not sung.

The Sequence is obligatory only on Easter Sunday and Pentecost.

Using the new Lectionary

One of the hallmarks of the new Sunday Lectionary, as indeed of the new Order of the Mass, is variety.

It is true that the reading of all three scripture passages is highly recommended. But it may be felt that the people need considerable preparation for this. If a choice between the First and Second Readings is to be made, what criteria should be used?

The main thing to aim at is that the people should understand the scriptures as a whole, so that the fundamental criterion will be the harmony of the First or Second Reading with the Gospel. Sometimes, as in Advent or Lent, the Old Testament reading will be more in keeping with the Gospel, as it points to the main stages in God's preparation of his people for the gift of salvation. At other times of the year, the reading of the Old Testament is less important, but if it is read, it should be continued over a number of weeks, so that the change to the Second Reading comes at the time when a new Epistle is started. Then the Epistle should be read semi-continuously for the set number of weeks. The spirit of the Lectionary is against the constant omission of Old Testament passages and against chopping and changing from First to Second Reading each alternate week.

The variety permitted in the use of the Responsorial Psalm and Response should not mean that the same Psalm and same Response are used for months on end. The people will need some time to get used to the Responses, but they are sufficiently short to be learnt quite easily.

Letting the congregation know

To prevent rigidity on the one hand, and chaos on the other, a common policy in a diocese, deanery or parish is going to be needed. The possible variations in the Mass now would seem to make it imperative that the people are informed as to which of the variable parts are going to be used. There is a possibility of a number of introductory greetings and penitential acts; a choice of Readings, Responsorial Psalms and Refrains, Alleluias, Prefaces, Canons and Acclamations after the Consecration. A good solution would probably be to utilize the Hymn Board that exists in a good many parishes to inform the congregation about the variable parts. The parish bulletin could be useful in this respect, as it could safeguard continuity and consistency. Last but not least, the information can be given by word of mouth at the beginning of Mass, if not by a lector, by the priest himself.

Many doubt that liturgical reform will be the cure to all ills. Yet as the spirit of the liturgy promotes an increase in knowledge of Christ's message and a deeper prayer, thanking God for his supreme gift, it may cure quite a few of our ills. The spirit of the liturgy will promote the spirit of intelligent preparation and variation for the mystery which is the centre of Christian life.

We hope this book will furnish the information and direction to help priest and teacher find their way around the new Lectionary, and be a useful companion to the pocket-sized edition[1] of this vital link in the reform of Christian worship.

[1] *People's Pocket Lectionary for Sundays, Year Two*, Geoffrey Chapman 1969.

Introductions to Books Frequently Used in the Lectionary for Year Two

1. THE BOOK OF ISAIAH

Of all the Old Testament Books, pride of place in the liturgy belongs to the Book of Isaiah. Its sublime doctrine on the Messiah and the Suffering Servant of God makes it a natural choice for the Advent preparation for Christmas and the Lenten prelude to Holy Week. The revised Mass readings continue the ancient tradition assigning readings from the Prophecy of Isaiah to Advent. Isaiah is more a Gospel than a Prophecy, remarks Jerome. It leads the collection of Old Testament prophets more for its religious importance and beauty than for its age and size.

A prophet is not specially inspired to foresee the future. He is God's appointed mouthpiece to his people. To interpret Isaiah, or indeed any of the prophets, it is crucial to grasp the historical backcloth to his work. The super-powers and block-politics of the day seep into the book. Above all, the prophet points out God's views on current affairs and his absolute control over them. Isaiah is perhaps the greatest of the prophetic spokesmen whose words have come down to us in writing.

Yet the Book of Isaiah is more than an anthology of the prophet's sayings. It is rather the record of centuries-long Isaian tradition. The larger part of the book is in fact devoted to the ministry of the eighth century prophet called Isaiah (chapters 1–39), but the second half is the work of a disciple or several disciples writing about the time of Israel's exile in Babylonia two centuries later.

First Isaiah, the eighth century prophet

In the awesome vision described in chapter six, Isaiah puts his prophetic calling in the year King Uzziah died (742 BC), and for the next forty years his voice was heard above the international clamour that shook Jerusalem.

For two hundred years the chosen people had been divided into separate kingdoms. During Isaiah's youth, the northern kingdom of Israel and his native Judah to the south enjoyed almost unparalleled peace and prosperity. At the time of his calling this was changed. The conquering armies of Assyria, a state far to the north-east of Palestine, dominated the minds and hearts of the people he addressed. Just as the sea fascinates any land-locked nation, so the Mediterranean fascinated the Assyrians and their line of brilliant king-generals. Palestinian states blocking their march west were overrun one by one. The northern kingdom of Israel was completely destroyed in 722 BC and her people deported.

After this disaster to Israel, politics in Jerusalem, Judah's capital, spelt intrigue and counter-intrigue between pro-Assyrian and pro-Egyptian factions. The result, despite continual warnings and threats from Isaiah, was a Jerusalem crippled with an enormous fine and the rest of Judah ruined and desolate. Isaiah's death? One tradition tells us he was martyred under the avidly pro-Assyrian king, Manasseh.

Isaiah's *message* was coloured very much by his vocation-vision. Revealed to Isaiah was the great holiness and transcendence of Yahweh, God of the Fathers; in contrast to this divine holiness was man's sinfulness. Especially the pride and injustice of Judah called for Yahweh's judgment and punishment. God is not the helpless spectator of a man-directed history, but its complete and absolute master. The Holy One of Israel is determined to have his people's faith and trust—the 'remnant' of Jerusalem and Sion are to be saved. A worthy successor to King David will teach God's ways and rule in true justice and peace.

Second Isaiah, the sixth century prophet of the Exile

Assyria's century-old empire sank before the armies of her southern neighbour, Babylon. Revolts in Judah occasioned, in

597 and 587 BC, two deportations that depopulated the land of its rulers, chief citizens and craftsmen. The exiles brought to Babylonia were in despair, longing in vain for a speedy return to their country. But their hopes were fanned by the news that Cyrus the king of Persia and Media had begun to press southwards against the Babylonian empire. A decade later, Cyrus took Babylon and decreed the restoration of Jerusalem; the exiles could go home.

Directing the hope and prayers for that return was an unknown prophet we call Second Isaiah. In contrast to the terse lyricism of the earlier prophet, Second Isaiah's songs are more solemn, expansive and even repetitive, as he re-echoes and develops the Isaian themes of hope and promise. His *Book of the Consolation of Israel* (Isaiah 40–55) can be sign-posted with such titles as Monotheist, Messianist and Universalist. He has imbibed the history of his people, Abraham, Moses and the Exodus, David and Jerusalem. Yahweh, their God, is Lord of this history, governing all by his Word. As invincibly as his all-powerful Word created the universe, he will faithfully and gloriously carry out his promises to his people. Second Isaiah's theological skill thus united unequivocally God's purpose in creation with the worldwide mission of his chosen people.

The Servant Songs

Set into Second Isaiah's work are four beautiful *Songs of the Servant of Yahweh*.[1] The prophet's words and expressions soar with new force into pinnacles of Old Testament revelation. He shifts his theme from God's works for his people, especially in a new Exodus, to a new vision. The ideal Israel finds perfect expression in an individual who embraces all the qualities of Israel's great men of the past. Endowed with the divine spirit, he instructs men in God's designs, he is abused and put to death, but his suffering will be for the salvation of all men and God will glorify him.

Is this figure merely an individualization of the people of Israel as a whole? It may well be, though the prophet expresses it in a quite singular way. For Jesus was able to apply the features of this Suffering Servant directly to himself and to his mission. Each

[1] Isaiah 42:1-9; 49:1-6; 50:4-11; 52:13–53:12.

evangelist soaked his Gospel with the character of this Servant. In fact, servant theology permeates the whole of the New Testament. The liturgy, like the New Testament, constantly recalls these remarkable songs in order to visualize and interpret the humiliation and glorification of Christ.

Third Isaiah, after the restoration

A change in perspective marks the final chapters of Isaiah (chapters 56–66). The return of the exiles began in 538 BC. Yet few made the journey. The New Temple took years to complete, and was a poor shadow of the structure gutted by the Babylonians seventy years before. Hostility from neighbours to the north and poverty within the community added to the feelings of gloom and despondency.

Though the return was not nearly so glorious as Second Isaiah had foretold, his vision is continued and his doctrine quoted by a disciple (or group of disciples) bent on adapting his preaching to the dismal post-exilic scene. Now the doctrine of hope and world-wide worship of Yahweh is gently sobered with ideas on purification and fidelity to God's will. Familiar canons of Judaism —Law, Sabbath and Temple—begin to take shape.

2. THE BOOK OF PSALMS

The religious message of the psalms is as kaleidoscopic as the religious message of the Old Testament itself, whose prayer book it is. God, the creator and saviour of his people, the Temple and its sacrificial liturgy are doctrines that stand out. All the varieties of human feelings and attitudes are here : the love of friends and of 'the just', the fear of perishing in the pit of Sheol, the Israelite hell, even passionate hatred of those who oppress and calumniate them.

Hebrew poetry

It is easy to forget that the psalms are poetry. We should at least be aware of the two essential features of Hebrew metre[1]

---

[1] Not unlike the English poet, the Hebrew poet groups unstressed syllables around a pattern of stressed or accented ones. After two to four of these

and parallelism. The metre is very difficult to convey in translations; some attempt it, but more often the printing arrangement marks only the beginning and end of the Hebrew poetic line.

More obvious in translation is the parallelism : the idea of the first part of the line is continued in the second part, with the same kind of word arrangement and meaning. For example :

> Why do the nations / conspire*
> and the peoples / plot in vain
> (Ps 2:1)

Verses have normally between three and five lines; but occasionally we find much longer verses of twenty-two lines, based on the twenty-two letters of the alphabet.

The poet's skill is shown in the manipulating of metre, parallelism and verse length. There is a great danger of the monotony often felt in the very long alphabetic Ps 118.

Types of psalms

The Hebrew title for the Book of Psalms is 'Songs of Praise'. But in fact not all of the Psalms are songs of praise. There are three main types : hymns of praise, psalms of thanksgiving, and psalms of lament or petition. As we might expect, this last group is the largest by far, especially psalms of petition addressed by an individual to God, which comprise one-third of the Psalter.

Choice of psalms

A variety of motives govern the choice of a psalm as the Responsorial Psalm of a given Mass.
1. The quoting of a psalm in the First or Second Reading of the Mass means this psalm will be used.

---

stressed syllables there is a pause or caesura; then another two to four stressed syllables terminated by an end-stop, giving a line of poetry, which is also a sentence or idea unit. Normally there are 3 + 3 stressed syllables per line (i.e. three stressed syllables with accompanying unstressed ones, caesura, then three more stressed syllables, lastly the end-stop); but variations such as 3 + 2 (the Lamentation metre), 4 + 4, and even the elongated 3 + 3 + 3 (another caesura and three stressed syllables inserted before the end-stop) are frequent.

2. Similarly, if the Gospel quotes a psalm, that psalm is used.
3. Similarity of language between the First Reading and a particular psalm will lead to its choice.
4. Contacts of message and mood between the Readings as a whole and a particular psalm will likewise lead to its selection; for example Ps 22 'The Lord is my shepherd' for Good Shepherd Sunday (the Fourth Sunday of Paschaltide).
5. Psalms associated by liturgical tradition with special seasons are retained in these seasons.
6. Any other psalms, not already chosen under one of the first five headings, may be selected for the remaining Masses.

If psalms in addition to those set by the Lectionary are sung, how are they to be chosen? Attention should be paid to the content and mood of the psalm, its literary type, and the six criteria mentioned above. A psalm or popular hymn which cuts across the mood of the celebration should be avoided. A good alternative selection is available in *The Simple Gradual*.

3.　THE GOSPEL ACCORDING TO ST MARK

A Gospel

Any writer would shudder at the thought of his work being submitted to the kind of scrutiny the Gospels receive. However, some rough handling has made the Gospels emerge in more profound simplicity and rugged beauty.

Unfortunately it has not always been obvious that a Gospel is not a history nor a biography, but the Good News, a testimony of the faith of the community for which it was written. The community's interests did not invent or suppress, but selected for preservation the Lord Jesus' words and works, as they had been taught them. Save for the Passion story, the early Christians seem to have been surprisingly uninterested in being given a universal clock or Esso maps of Palestine. Once they knew the general plan of Jesus' public life, details of days, months and years were allowed to slip. Much more important to their faith was the *meaning* of who he was and what he did. Thus the early apostolic witness was intent on preaching the meaning of what was really happening in the events of Jesus' life and work.

Who originated the idea of *writing* a Gospel may always remain a mystery. Was it a Gospel-school led by the apostle Matthew? Or a brainwave of the disciple Mark who hit on the idea of prefacing the Passion story with a long theological introduction to explain why the Passion happened? What has to be thoroughly grasped is that each evangelist has a definite theological plan behind his compilation of stories and sayings, and that St Mark's is undoubtedly the first of the four canonical Gospels to be written.

Mark the Evangelist

The early Church is unanimous in attributing the second Gospel to Mark. He is described by the second century bishop, Papias, as 'the interpreter of Peter', carefully writing down what Peter preached. There is a Mark with Peter in Rome (1 Peter 5:13). So opinion has it that Mark wrote in Rome just before or not long after Peter's martyrdom there about 64 AD. Modern commentators generally date this Gospel in the decade 65–75 AD and often identify this Mark with the John Mark who accompanied Paul.

Mark's purpose

Is Mark's Gospel a jumble of short episodes? Did he really plan his work very well? The Gospel would stand up poorly to 'a life-story must have a proper time sequence' criterion. It is true that we do get a general ground-plan of the life of Jesus: his baptism, mission in Galilee, journey to Jerusalem, Jerusalem ministry, Passion, etc.; it is very tempting to feel that Mark builds the account around these headings. But the Gospel is better seen as the *message of faith* constructed on a plan whose very arrangement clearly shows Mark's brilliant theological portrait of Jesus' person and work.

With mounting drama and irony, Mark presents Jesus firstly as the Messiah and then as the Suffering Servant, paralleling this with the misunderstanding and disbelief of his hearers, and the slow faltering steps in faith of the disciples who so often show such dim-witted incomprehension.

The two stage plan

Stage One. Thoroughly respecting the Old Testament message that God's kingdom or reign was to come through the Messiah, his anointed, Mark begins the first part of his Gospel by introducing Jesus preaching 'the Gospel of God' : 'The time is fulfilled, and the kingdom of God is at hand; repent, and believe in the Gospel' (Mk 1:14,15). Jesus' proclamation that the kingdom of God is near is articulated as he begins the destruction of Satan's kingdom. All physical as well as all moral evils were the manifestation of Satan's rule in the world. But Jesus still enjoins silence on the unclean spirits and hides his Messiahship because of the close association of God's kingdom with his death and resurrection, as yet in the future.

Particularly injurious to Jesus' teaching was the popular expectation of the Messiah as a nationalistic figure. He calls for personal, interior repentance and renewal, since it is in the heart that Satan reigns more than in the national, political situation. The ministry of Jesus, in Mark's view, united the coming of God's kingdom, the defeat of Satan and revelation about himself; it is met with almost total misunderstanding.

Two multiplications of bread, prefiguring the Messianic Banquet, and the miracle of the blind man at Bethsaida, symbolizing a step of the disciples on the road to faith, set the scene for the hinge of the Gospel : Jesus asks, 'Who do men say that I am?' Peter replies, 'You are the Christ' (Mk 8:27,29). This first confession of Jesus' Messiahship by his disciples (in the mouth of Peter) completes the first part of the Gospel and introduces the second.

Stage Two. Immediately after these words of Peter, Mark has the disciples once more stupified :

> And he began to teach them that the Son of Man was destined to suffer grievously, to be rejected by the elders and the chief priests and the scribes, and to be put to death, and after three days to rise again; and he said all this quite openly (Mk 8:31-32).

Jesus is not the Messiah they think he is, but 'openly' has the role of God's Suffering Servant. From now on in the Gospel, miracles are fewer, preaching to the crowds rarer; Jesus takes his disciples apart and instructs them privately, and the Markan narrative takes him on his journey to Jerusalem, punctuating the journey with two more announcements of his coming sufferings and resurrection. The cure of the blind Bartimaeus at Jericho is another symbol of the disciples' progression in faith, but the heightening Servant motif emphasizes Jesus' aloneness as the Saviour who is to suffer for all men. Unbelief brings down the judgment of Jesus, in deed and word.

The climax comes when Jesus openly claims a Messiahship of divine dimension before the High Priest. He is condemned and suffers alone, but his death brings the old covenant to an end as the temple veil is torn down the middle, and the new world begins on the centurion's lips, 'Truly this man was the Son of God!' (Mk 15:39).

Mark in the new Lectionary

Mark has skilfully woven the traditional preaching of Peter and the community into the drama of the mystery of Jesus. Mark is a theological giant. With depth and simplicity, he conveys to us what the Gospel really means: the revelation of Jesus as the Christ in word and deed is the event that brings our salvation.

The new Lectionary gives ample scope for the preacher to give Mark the credit that is his due and to unfold his plan to the people. In Year Two, on the Sundays throughout the Year there is continuous reading of almost the entire Gospel. There are readings from Mark also on the first two Sundays of Advent and Lent in Year Two, but Mark yields to John at the end of Lent and during Paschaltide (except for the Feast of the Ascension) and is supplemented by John from 17th–21st Sunday throughout the Year, because of Mark's brevity. Chapter six of St John is thus inserted into the corresponding Loaves Section in Mark.

4. THE GOSPEL ACCORDING TO ST JOHN

For the scholar, the Gospel of St John bristles with a century and a half of problems. But no lack of certainty has impoverished the magnificence of this document of faith called from early times the 'spiritual' Gospel, and its author 'the theologian'.

John and his Gospel

The New Testament itself gives an occasional inkling of the importance of the apostle John in the early Church. The authority of his preaching would need to be great to safeguard the acceptance of a Gospel tradition differing so enormously from that of the other evangelists.

Even early tradition indicates a process of composition for the Fourth Gospel that is rather more complicated than a simple dictation straight from John's mouth of what he saw and heard. John's disciples played a large part in bringing the Gospel to light. It seems likely that John's preaching was stereotyped for his disciples, being put into writing about the time Matthew and Luke wrote their Gospels (about 75 AD). But only after one or several editions (under direct or indirect supervision of the apostle) did the Gospel find its final form, probably just after John had died (Ephesus 95–100 AD).

John's originality

Why is John so different? Some take it for granted that he was influenced by a tradition other than the 'normal' Christian one (of St Mark's Gospel). Great ingenuity has been used to prove John borrowed from pagan philosophy and heretical theologies, perhaps copying some of these sources.

However, it is unnecessary to look outside normal Jewish traditions for things that influenced him, in particular the rabbinical speculations on Old Testament Wisdom literature. Besides, the Fourth Gospel's author clearly has great theological talent. Fifty years of Christian preaching and reflexion bolster his language and formulations. Even though the Gospel was composed primarily for strengthening the faith of Christians, the author shows no desire to ignore the religious language and ideas of his day.

John's intention

A solemn sacral style with a care in language bordering on the technical; personal asides of the evangelist in his narrative; an eye to symbolism in the events he recalls; the very selectivity that went into the Gospel's making : all these point to careful planning that justifies calling John 'the theologian'.

His purpose is unambiguous :

> There were many other signs that Jesus worked and the disciples saw, but they are not recorded in this book. These are recorded so that you may believe that Jesus is the Christ, the Son of God, and that believing you may have life through his name (Jn 20:30-31).

These verses are crystal clear in telling us what to expect as key points in this Gospel : faith and the testimony that provokes it, life with its associated ideas of love and joy. But the kingpin is going to be Jesus of Nazareth, the Messiah-Christ and the Son of God, who is testifier and object of this faith, and the source of this life.

John's Gospel lends itself so magnificently to homily themes on faith, love, truth, sin, symbolism, sacraments and so on. But to treat these in isolation could well distort John's clear intention of rooting every passage into the person of Jesus.

The plan carried out

John's vision is so much his own. Yet we see a twofold tendency in John similar to the approach of Mark. Firstly, Jesus is the Messiah, the Christ. We could call this a horizontal view. Jesus is inserted into salvation history as God's promised anointed, sent to suffer and save. John selects messianic signs and stresses messianic kingship even in the Passion narratives. Secondly, a vertical viewpoint presents Jesus as the Son of God and one with his Father, an aspect more emphasized in certain discourses and in the resurrection accounts.

Unlike Mark who unites his twofold theme under the Servant

Saviour motif, John links them under the theme of Jesus as Revealer. Jesus' revelation is preparatory and incomplete in the first part of the Gospel (chapters 1–12), but final and total in his 'Hour' of glorification (chapters 13–21). For John the 'Hour' of glorification is the cross, *the* work of Jesus and his Father, the unique event encompassing passion, death, resurrection, ascension and imparting of the Spirit. Though John's faith is in the glorified Jesus, the crucifixion and glorification did not come out of the blue. John witnessed the preparation for it when Jesus presented in his public life who he was and what he was about. In the face of the revelation about Jesus' person, indifference is impossible; men must either believe or reject him.

Part One.   The Prologue is an overture to the Gospel's message and themes. Then, after introducing the witness of John the Baptist and the first of Jesus' disciples, John leans firstly towards the messianic side of Jesus' revelation (chapters 2–4) and then towards the Sonship aspect (chapters 5-9).

In the messianic section, two revelation signs, the New Wine (at the wedding feast of Cana) and the New Temple (in the cleansing of the Temple), accompany three degrees of faith : in Nicodemus, faith is only in signs; the Samaritan woman has faith in Jesus' words; but the ruler of the synagogue simply believes without strings when Jesus requests faith.

Similarly, the Son of God section begins with two revelation signs, the cure of the cripple at the pool, and the multiplication of the loaves. But this time a discourse explains and develops each sign, about the works of Jesus and the bread of life.

In the context of the Jewish great feasts, John shows Jesus revealing his superiority over the founders of the Jewish religion, Abraham and Moses. Unbelief and hatred pursue him. The cure of the blind man given 'light', followed by the good shepherd discourse about Jesus' own, causes a 'division among the Jews' (10:19). He tells them openly that he is the Son of God in a unique way. For John the journey to the cross has started (chapters 11–12). His hour of glorification approaches, when he will become the resurrection and the life to everyone as he was for Lazarus; he will draw all things to himself and vindicate his true Messiahship. In words that hark back to the Prologue, John ends the first part of his Gospel on a note of judgment on those who have rejected Jesus.

Part Two. His Hour now come, Jesus turns to his own. In deed and word he teaches them to be united with him in life, love and service. This union with Jesus is to be brought about by the Spirit who is to come through his glorification.

John sees the cross as a throne of triumph. From it Jesus completes his Father's work and gives up the Spirit, as blood and water (the eucharist and baptism) flow into his own, the Church. The risen glorified Jesus can breathe the Spirit into his disciples to send them out in his name, as the Father had sent him.

The very way John put his Gospel together underlines Jesus' *presence* in the Church through the Spirit, a presence in sign and sacrament, liturgy and charity. Not the presence of a spiritual 'force' but of a person who though glorified continues to live as the man John saw, heard and touched, Jesus of Nazareth, son of the Mary entrusted to him, who was and is all the while God's eternal Son.

John's Gospel in the new Lectionary

Unlike the other evangelists, John has no special year of his own. Readings from his Gospel are spaced over the three years of the cycle.

John is the evangelist of Lent and Paschaltide. The Church sees in the great signs and discourses of the Fourth Gospel the mysterious depths of her own existence, and reads this spiritual Gospel especially at the time she is celebrating the central events of her salvation. From the Third Sunday of Lent, we hear the sign of the cleansing of the Temple, the dialogue with Nicodemus, the discourse on the grain of wheat (with the option every year of the dialogue with the Samaritan woman, the cure of the blind man and the raising of Lazarus). The Holy Thursday, Good Friday (John's Passion) and Easter Sunday Gospels are from John. And throughout Paschaltide the discourses about Jesus' own are heard. The tradition of reading the Prologue of St John at the Day Mass of Christmas is continued.

From the second century, the Church has recognized that it

is St John's Gospel that has given her the deepest spiritual answer to the question 'Who is Jesus?'.

5. THE ACTS OF THE APOSTLES

On the Sundays from Easter to Pentecost, Old Testament readings are replaced by passages from the Acts of the Apostles. This continues the liturgical custom of many rites, which can claim support not just from tradition but from the theological character of the second book of St Luke.

St Luke's Acts

Though the title 'Acts of . . .' has pagan precedents in books like 'The Acts of Alexander the Great', it is clearly not intended that the Acts of the Apostles should be a history of the mission of the twelve apostles. Nor is it an apology for Paul's mission to the Gentiles, as is sometimes claimed.

Besides the great care Luke uses in the handling of his sources, his skilful historical sense and his ability with the Greek language, he seems deliberately to imitate the Old Testament style of things, especially the theological bent of the Old Testament histories.

Luke is the theologian of salvation history. For him the Old Testament is both a panorama and pattern of God's dealings with men. It is also the preparation for the greatest act of God, the universal salvation brought about in the death and resurrection of his Son. After describing this great act in the Gospel, he brings his theological sights to bear on the expansion of the mission commanded by the risen Lord. Hence the Acts of the Apostles is a vision of the life and mission of the Church from its apostolic nucleus to its expansion to the ends of the earth, symbolized in its reaching Rome. It is an idyllic account of God's final age.

The Book of Acts is thus eminently suitable for the Church's attention on the Sundays of Paschaltide, as she celebrates the effects of Christ's resurrection, ascension and gift of the Holy Spirit, the mysteries responsible for her very existence.

The Gospel of the Spirit

More than once the Old Testament underscores the inspiration and direction given to the chosen people by the spirit of God.

Luke spots this and makes the guidance of the Spirit a cornerstone of his own viewpoint.

Not only is the conception of Jesus caused by the Spirit, but the whole life of Jesus is continually dominated by the Spirit. After the resurrection the Spirit comes into his own. More than anything else, Acts is the story of the Holy Spirit guiding the infant Church. The Spirit promotes the proclamation and faith in the saving words and deeds of the Lord, which begin from the apostolic preaching in Jerusalem, reach through to Judea and Samaria and out to the ends of the earth.

The position and privileges of the Holy City, so marked in the Old Testament, are also continued in Luke's Gospel. Jesus comes into Jerusalem as an infant, journeys there through half the Gospel, is put to death there and there rises from the dead. Acts continues to see Jerusalem as the centre of the Church's life and mission. Starting from Jerusalem, the Word goes out to the ends of the earth.

A third dominant attitude of Luke, begun in his Gospel but rooted in the Old Testament, is his interest in the poor and outcast to illustrate that Christ came for all men. The Jewish people, though privileged and blessed by God in the Old Testament, have occasioned the preaching of the Gospel to the Gentiles by their rejection of Jesus and persecution of his chosen witnesses. The universalism promised in the Old Testament and preached by Jesus is now realized.

Luke has it in mind to show converts from paganism that God's full plan is now in operation. The Spirit of God is poured out to all the peoples of the earth, who now look up to Jerusalem as Mother of all the Churches.

Luke's plan in Acts

As the keynote of Acts is the Church's mission, it is not surprising to find a geographical pattern in a work of theological history. Luke may idealize this mission, but the idealizing does depend on real events :

It is not for you to know times or dates that the Father has decided by his own authority, but you will receive power when the Holy Spirit comes on you, and then you will

be my witnesses not only in Jerusalem but throughout
Judaea and Samaria, and indeed to the ends of the earth
(Acts 1:7-8).

Notice that Christ insists on the completion of the Church's
mission before the final victory in his Second Coming. The
attitude of the early Church towards the Second Coming of Christ
is seen clearly in the early letters of St Paul. They really thought
he was coming back very soon. But as years went by and he did
not return, they had to justify it theologically. John did it, for
example, by stressing Christ's continued presence; Luke, on the
other hand, devised a theology of mission. In both these views
the Holy Spirit plays a crucial part.

Once the Holy Spirit is given to the little flock at Pentecost, the
apostles are absolutely clear on the job ahead. They preach and
are opposed by the authorities. Still the Church progresses; Luke
stresses this in three progress reports. The death of Stephen signals
the expansion to the rest of Palestine and occasions the introduction of Saul, who under his Greek name Paul will fulfil the world-
wide mission.

The Gentile mission begins, however, with Peter's mission
to Cornelius the Centurion who lived in the pagan coastal
town of Caesarea. The legitimacy of such a mission is assured as
the Holy Spirit falls upon the household of Cornelius in the
Pentecost of the Gentiles. The Apostolic Council confirms the
universal mission and the break with Judaism. Luke sees in Paul
the chief instrument of the mission to the ends of the earth in
which he himself took part. When Paul arrives in Rome, the hub
of the world they knew, the command of the Lord is complete.
Once in Rome the Word virtually fills the earth.

In the Lectionary

The Acts of the Apostles can thus be a splendid preparation
for Pentecost, from which the Church had its origin. Acts is the
book of the Spirit. Its discourses, though so Lucan, capture those
early days of enthusiasm brought by the Holy Spirit, and occur
at important points in the Church's expansion. These discourses
are consequently passages of importance for the liturgy, and so
too are the progress reports which describe the unity and energy
of the early mother community.

In Year Two, besides the accounts of the Ascension and Pentecost, five readings are devoted to Peter's preaching, especially the Sermon to Cornelius in chapter ten.

6. THE FIRST LETTER OF ST PAUL TO THE CORINTHIANS

Paul's letters to the Corinthian Church

The Corinth of St Paul's day was a wealthy and populous port. In spite of the reputation of Corinthian morals, the Church Paul founded there during his eighteen month stay (50–51 AD) was numerous. Paul seems to have loved this community as a parent loves a rather troublesome child; though passionately devoted to its new-found faith, it was not noted for its obedience to Paul's directions.

Paul wrote at least four letters to the Corinthians :

Letter A : before our present First Corinthians
Letter B : First Corinthians, written about Easter 57 AD
Letter C : a letter 'written in tears', about Pentecost 57
Letter D : Second Corinthians, a month or two later.

Some authors see 2 Cor 6:14–7:1 as (part of) Letter A, and 2 Cor 10–13 as Letter D.

We know nothing of the circumstances of Letter A. Letter B, our First Corinthians, was written at the end of Paul's mission in Ephesus, about Easter 57 AD.

Three motives led him to write this long letter, the most pastoral of all his epistles. Firstly, Chloe's people (1 Cor 1:11) reported trouble in the community—rivalry and factions. Secondly, the Corinthians had sent questions to Paul through three of their members, Stephanas, Fortunatus and Achaicus (1 Cor 16:17). Thirdly, these three messengers reported further abuses in Corinth. Stephanas and his companions probably took the letter back with them to Corinth.

After their departure, more drastic developments were reported. This time a letter was not sufficient, so before the Pentecost of 57 AD Paul set out for Greece. One or several of the Corinthian community, or perhaps some new arrivals, started to attack Paul's rights as their apostolic founder. This was guaranteed to upset him. So he hurried to the city to sort matters out. Grossly insulted there, he left in disgust, perhaps also to prevent the community being torn apart. He then wrote to them in anger and sorrow (Letter C). The letter had the desired effect. Second Corinthians (Letter D), written perhaps a month or two later, is more gentle and conciliatory, though still showing something of his anger against those who dared to affront his personal authority and message.

A difficult mission

Both (surviving) letters to the Corinthians reveal the difficult context of Paul's mission to them. They had not been Christians so very long. They were proud of their Greek heritage, especially intellectual autonomy. Submission to apostolic authority was extremely difficult for them. They were vulnerable to 'Judaizing' preachers, who claimed Christianity must remain rooted in the observance of the Jewish Law and traditions. Paul denied the Law any such claim over Christians. Who were they to believe?

For Paul there is only one solution. As their father and founder, they must accept him as the true spokesman of the Gospel. Christ had appointed Paul as their apostle. No one else might claim their allegiance. And the only Gospel they had heard from him was that salvation comes through Christ's cross.

The message of First Corinthians

First Corinthians involves itself in a host of questions. The community's basic difficulty was factionism. They felt they could choose their own religious leaders and relied on worldly wisdom to govern their Christian life. The result was a rivalry that made use of pagan law-courts, and a permissiveness that allowed gross sexual laxity. Paul deals with these troubles in the first part of the letter (chapters 1–6).

He comes to the questions put to him by the Corinthians in the second part of the letter (chapters 7–15). They have problems of marriage and virginity; they were worried about the use of meat known to have been offered to idols, yet on sale in the public market; there were disorders in the liturgy and quarrelling about the gifts of the Spirit; and a very serious difficulty about the resurrection from the dead.

All these matters worried Paul very much. It is no wonder that he had to pack his bags so soon after he sent this letter. But even the most serious turn of events could be solved with the principle Paul outlined in the letter : Christians must be submissive to the Gospel message and to the authority it gave to its authentic witnesses. Only in Second Corinthians do we find the full-blooded, no-nonsense defence of Paul's position.

In the Lectionary

The pastoral nature of the letter comes out in its use in the Lectionary. Sections of it are read semi-continuously in all three years of the cycle.

Immediately after the Christmas season, we have readings from First Corinthians. In Year Two, there are five readings, taken from chapters 6–11, beginning on the First Sunday throughout the Year. (In Years One and Three, eight consecutive readings begin on the same Sunday.) In these chapters Paul discusses sexual behaviour, marriage and virginity, the question of meat offered to idols and liturgical misconduct.

This section of the letter is sufficient to illustrate the burning zeal and pastoral concern of Paul. Better than any other letter, First Corinthians reveals Paul in action.

7. THE LETTER OF ST PAUL TO THE EPHESIANS

Encyclical letter from Rome

Paul spent nearly three years in his evangelization of Ephesus, from the autumn of 54 AD to the spring of 57. Luke recounts some of the events of that mission in the Asia Minor capital in Acts 19–20.

The Ephesian Church is certainly a likely addressee of a letter from Paul, yet practically every circumstance about this letter has been queried. Did Paul write it during the Roman captivity? Was it really to the Ephesians? Is it Pauline at all?

Being in Rome, capital of the world, could very easily provoke the captive Paul to consider the Church as universal, and look again at the position of Christ. Hence Ephesians, a synthetic exposition of Paul's renewed thinking about Christ and the Church.

It is best to see Ephesians as an Encyclical Letter addressed to all the Churches of the Asia Province rather than solely to the community at Ephesus. It was probably taken East by a certain Tychicus, who carried the letter to the Colossians and the note to Philemon at the same time.

Paul often used a secretary to help him with his letters. He might well have left the man considerable freedom in the actual formulation of Ephesians. It would at least explain certain difficulties of style and language.

Ephesians and Romans

It is interesting to compare the similarity of Galatians and Romans with Colossians and Ephesians. Galatians is a polemic against teachers attempting to turn Paul's converts to Jewish practices. Colossians similarly attacks those trying to lead the faithful astray with celestial mythologies, angel worship and false ideas on revelation, salvation and Christian knowledge. On the other hand, Romans takes up the doctrine of Galatians and weaves it into a systematic treatment of Paul's teaching on justification and salvation through faith. In a parallel way, Ephesians takes up the polemical questions of Colossians and utilizes even the vocabulary of the false teachers to form a new synthesis of doctrine on Christ, Head of the Church, and the salvation that comes from the deep knowledge of this mystery. Christian knowledge, unlike the knowledge proclaimed by the false teachers, must include doctrinal and moral commitment to Christ.

Ephesians shows an evolution in Paul's thought. In Romans, the Gospel is the Proclamation, the Message that is God's power to justify and sanctify those who accept it. Ephesians modifies the perspective. The Gospel is God's secret plan now revealed in Christ, producing through the Holy Spirit a new sanctifying awareness, or knowledge, in the man of faith.

In a word: if the Gospel is Christ's message of truth, Romans talks about it as message, Ephesians looks at it more as truth.

The message of Ephesians

Ephesians is a prayerful letter. It contains a long hymn of praise in chapter one, and a hymn of thanksgiving in chapter three. Paul may have deliberately adopted a liturgical style to make the letter more suitable for reading in liturgical assembly.

The opening Hymn of Praise (Eph 1:3-14) outlines the doctrine of the Epistle, especially verses 9-10 :

> He has let us know the mystery of his purpose, the hidden plan he so kindly made in Christ from the beginning to act upon when the times had run their course to the end : that he would bring everything together under Christ, as head, everything in the heavens and everything on earth.

God's work has universal scope. God has revealed and achieved his plan for creation in Christ, who is now the centre and corner-stone of the universe. Christ revealed God's mysterious plan to his chosen apostles and gave them the Spirit to make it known to all men. (Paul prays in gratitude for *his* commission from Christ.) He has broken down the division between the Jews and the rest of men. In fact, it was God's plan from the beginning to build all men into a heavenly temple, a single people with Christ as head. The man who has accepted Christ's revelation and entered his new community lives now as a new creature. He renounces immoral behaviour that breaks the unity of charity and holiness, which Christ is founding among all mankind; for 'we are God's work of art, created in Christ Jesus to live the good life, as from the beginning he had meant us to live it' (Eph 2:10).

So Paul sees Christians as members of one total world-wide community, the Universal Church. Just as the mystery of God is made visible through Christ, in whom the fullness of the divinity is made manifest, so the mystery of Christ is made visible in its fullness in his Church. Small wonder the Church, in her worship, has always treasured an Epistle which shows so sublimely the core of her existence.

In the Lectionary

The time for the semi-continuous reading of the Epistle to the Ephesians is in Year Two, on seven Sundays throughout the

Year, beginning on the fifteenth. But on all three years of the cycle, passages from the Ephesians are read on the first Sunday of the calendar year, on the Epiphany, the Ascension and the Feast of the Sacred Heart.

8. THE FIRST EPISTLE OF ST JOHN

The author

In spite of the differences of emphasis between John's Gospel and his First Epistle, the ideas and language are so close that many see the Letter as a commentary on the Gospel. The Letter would hardly be intelligible without a knowledge of the Gospel.

The introduction and conclusion normally found in New Testament letters are lacking. This could be explained if First John is seen as an Encyclical Letter to the Churches of Asia, sent out with Second and Third John as covering notes to specific Churches.

The message

On many points the doctrine of First John is less developed than the Gospel's. 'Last Day' ideas are more in relief, in contrast to the Gospel's view of Christ as continually present to his Church. The title 'Paraclete' is reserved for the Holy Spirit in the Gospel, whereas Jesus is called 'paraclete' in the Epistle. There is more stress on Christ as expiation and sacrifice in First John; the Gospel sees everything under the aspect of Christ glorified in his hour.

The Epistle's terminology is less organic than the Gospel's; typical words like faith, light, love, sin, and commandment are manipulated to move the Epistle forward in a cyclic or spiral motion, rather like waves splashing the same shore but gradually creeping forward. But how these terms are slotted into a total Christian viewpoint is not clear. They do have a coherent pattern in the Gospel, but we are not sure John intended this same pattern in the Epistle.

The plan

The letter is obviously full of moral exhortation. However, for

John, Christian life and work are so intensely bound up with faith, that good works become *the* work, that is, faith in Christ. Complimentary to faith is love. Faith and love are the two sides of a coin we should call life. 'The Word, who is life—this is our subject' (1 Jn 1:1). To Christ's revelation, the response is faith; to his dedication to our salvation, the response is love; to the life that Christ lives, the response is a consciously lived Christian commitment. The result is a total union with God that makes us his children, together with the Son.

In no way does the treatment of one aspect of Christian life in the Epistle exclude the other aspects. John looks at one side of the coin first; he talks about living in the light, the truth, the Christian faith. Then he presents the other side, living as God's children in a union of love. But various conditions have to be met; there must be a break with sin; obedience given to God's commandments, especially the new commandment of love; worldly attitudes abandoned and false teachers denied. A final part considers love and faith in relation to each other.

John writes for the same reason as he wrote his Gospel:

I have written all this to you
so that you who believe in the name of the Son of God
may be sure that you have eternal life (1 Jn 5:13).

In the Lectionary

Readings from First John in the Sunday Lectionary are set for the Paschaltide of Year Two. The Letter is meant to be read over six consecutive Sundays.

It is chosen for Paschaltide because the mood of the Letter is so consistent with the mood of the liturgical season. Life in union with Christ as God's children is especially relevant to the baptismal and unity themes of the paschal mysteries.

The Christmas Cycle

*1 Advent (30 November 1969) — Baptism of our Lord
(11 January 1970)*

THE SEASON OF ADVENT

Two characteristics mark the season of 'Coming'—the commemoration of the First Coming of Christ and the Preparation for his Second Coming. If in the past, the expectation of Christ as judge cast a penitential cloud over the season, this was not really intended. Looking forward to Christ is for the Christian a thing to rejoice about. So the mood of Advent should be one of joyful anticipation.

1. Throughout the four Sundays of Advent, it is left mainly to the Second Readings to convey the expectation that the Lord will return and make his Father's work complete. However, Christ's Second Coming is the special theme of the First Sunday. The keyword is 'Watch!', and this can remain a keyword of the whole season if the Second Readings are to be used and the First omitted. If a choice is to be made between the First and Second Readings, the Old Testament passages would fit better into the season. It can be left to the Gospel of the First Sunday to keep alive this theme of the Second Coming, and the First Readings can then be applied to the situation of the Church as she continues to wait for her Master.

There is a theological tension involved in talking about the Second *Coming* of Christ. Though the New Testament occasionally uses the word 'coming' about Christ's return, it more frequently talks about the 'appearing', 'revelation' or 'presence' of Christ, as if he was invisibly present all the time and just had to become visible. The New Testament does not really give a straight answer to this tension. So the preacher should hesitate to

32

do so. What will really *come* to pass will be the definitive renewal promised by God.

The time between the First and Second Coming is *our* time, the time of the Church's mission.

2. Four figures, remotely and proximately, dominate the preparation for Christmas: David and Isaiah, John the Baptist and Mary.

The promise to David of an eternal dynasty paves the way for the stress on the kingly character of the Messiah. The promise is heard in its original setting on the Fourth Sunday of Advent (First Reading). It thus sets the mood of the Sunday which is devoted to the proximate preparation for Christmas.

The prophecy of Isaiah, as it is better called (see the Introduction to Isaiah), is the traditional book of Advent. It is read on the first three Sundays. All Advent readings from it have the return of Israel from exile as the backcloth. Isaiah points in hopeful expectation, not to a human messianic figure, but to the presence of God himself. The second and third parts of the prophecy concentrate less on a Davidic Messiah than on the Kingship of God.

The role and preaching of John the Baptist appear in the Gospels of the Second and Third Sundays. In the mind of the evangelists, John is only a voice calling the nation to repentance in preparation for the coming of the Messiah. The mission of Second Isaiah casts its shadow on the Baptist's life. His function in the Gospels highlights the element of man's unworthiness in the face of any intervention of God on behalf of his people.

In spite of so much literature about our Lady, she has very little to say in the Gospels. But the greatest compliment in the Bible is paid her, and she answers in a perfect expression of humility. She symbolizes so much of what Advent is about. The Advent season can be one of joy because the time of waiting is now finished. Gabriel's words to Mary, and her acceptance, close the Old Testament era and begin the New.

The Season of Advent starts with the First Sunday of Advent (the Sunday nearest to 30 November) and finishes on 24 December, before the celebration of the Mass set for the Christmas Vigil.

The Liturgy of Advent can be summed up in those final words of the New Testament—'Come, Lord Jesus'.

The theme of the First Sunday is the Second Coming of Christ; St Paul prays, in the Second Reading, that his Corinthian converts will remain faithful until that Coming; the Gospel tells us to be on the alert; and Isaiah looks forward to the era of the Saviour which will end suffering and shower joys in a way even Christian people have still to experience.

FIRST READING (ISAIAH 63:16-17; 64:1. 3-8)

Oh, that you would tear the heavens open and come down

Though the theme of the Mass is the Second Coming of Christ, the liturgy does not divorce this from the prophetic visions of the first coming of the saviour. Isaiah is traditionally the prophet of the messianic age. The cry for God to come down is from Third Isaiah's Psalm on the Return of the People from Exile. God is praised for his past benefits. His greatest benefit to them happened when he formed them as his people at the Exodus from Egypt. Though he heaped untold blessings on them, they deserted him. So their enemies attacked and crushed them and their lives without God became dry and withered. The prophet begs for forgiveness and reconciliation—'Lord, you are our Father' is heard twice. He prays that God will again bring his Presence to his people. It will bring indescribable joys, for he is their redeemer and father and they the work of his hands.

THE RESPONSORIAL PSALM continues the mood of the First Reading, praying for rescue from enemies and restoration of God's blessings.

SECOND READING (1 CORINTHIANS 1:3-9)

We are waiting for our Lord Jesus Christ to be revealed

Paul begins most of his Letters with a Thanksgiving Section, in which he thanks God for the great blessings he has showered on his converts and prays for their final perseverance in the Christian life—expressed by such a phrase as 'until our Lord Jesus Christ appears'. A passage taken from the introduction to the First Letter to the Corinthians is more than suitable for the Advent liturgy. Isaiah prophesies great blessings in the messianic times. The Corinthians, more than any other of Paul's converts, receive the gifts of the Spirit, a proof, says Paul, of the tremendous effect the preaching of the Gospel had among them, and also a pledge that their faith in his message will continue until the Lord comes in his great day. Early Christian preaching recast the Old Testament prophecies of the Day of Yahweh (of judgment or of light) into the Day of the Lord, when Christ would be seen in power and glory. This Day was called Christ's *parousia*, his appearing or final coming; it can even be termed his presence. This is the object of Christian hope as Christ's new presence will fulfil and complete God's promise of an eternal union of love.

THIRD READING (MARK 13:33-37)

Stay awake, because you do not know when the master of the house is coming

'Be on your guard' is very much the theme, not only of the Gospel, but of the whole Eschatological Discourse of St Mark (in chapter 13). It is also an important motto for our attitude towards the Second Coming.

Several perspectives pervade this Discourse in Mark. He recognizes the traditional apocalyptical expressions about the Lord's Coming (expressions which talk about the final completion of God's cosmic plan in catastrophic terms), yet seems to answer the disciples' question 'When will this be?' with the moral exhortation to watchfulness. The disciples are warned to watch in Gethsemane, but fail to stay awake.

In the Reading, there is the veiled suggestion of the parable of the watchful steward, so noted in Luke. This is enough to typify the kind of alertness needed; an alertness that signifies engagement in the Lord's service while he is away. Is the Lord really absent? There still exists the tension surrounding the Second Coming and the Abiding Presence of Jesus.

Three themes suggest themselves for preaching. The Second Coming of Christ is a banner of hope, as his First Coming was hoped for in the centuries before his birth. It is a moral warning to be on guard; though the Lord suffered ignominy while on earth, his return will be far different 'on the clouds of heaven'. Lastly, the time of watchfulness is also the time of missionary activity, the opportunity to gather the harvest into the kingdom.

More important than the figure of Isaiah in the preparation for Christ's Coming is the prophetic precursor of Jesus, John the Baptist.

The Gospel of this Second Sunday and that of next Sunday are devoted to the mission of the Baptist, as he prepared the people of Israel to accept the awaited envoy of God. Always associated with John's mission was the prophetic calling of that greatest of exilic prophets, Second Isaiah, whose songs prepared the return of Israel to her homeland. The Second Epistle of Peter continues last Sunday's theme of watchful patience and good conduct, while we wait for the Day of God's Judgment.

FIRST READING (ISAIAH 40:1-5. 9-11)

Prepare a way for the Lord

'Console my people, console them' begins Second Isaiah's Prophecy, whence comes its title: the Book of the Consolation of Israel (Isaiah 40–55). The prophet sees in Jerusalem the embodiment of all people committed heart and soul to God. God's voice in his heavenly court commands the restoration of the people, the dawn of a new Exodus, a magnificent procession back to the Holy City. The voice of God speaks words of invincible power—now it will achieve a new and marvellous liberation, and a new interior joy and peace. The way is not just the processional way, but the new manner of life with heart faithful to God. Jerusalem is going to hear the glad tidings, and witness the redeeming presence of God. He rules them and carries them as their king and shepherd.

THE RESPONSORIAL PSALM has the salvation theme also. The divine favours, personified as Mercy, Faithfulness, Justice and Peace, will be imparted in the messianic age.

SECOND READING (2 PETER 3:8-14)

We are waiting for the new heavens and new earth

There is a delay in the Lord's Coming! Do not be caught unawares, like the people were at the Flood, replies Peter. The delay is because 'God is merciful and gracious, slow to anger and abounding in steadfast love and faithfulness' (Exodus 34:6). Time

36

is no object to the vastness of his providence; he stays his hand to give people time to repent.

Note that the only explicit scriptural basis for the idea of a final conflagration is found in this passage. This image entered Jewish apocalyptical tradition from eastern pagan sources. In preaching, we have to be wary of giving the impression that God's revelation demands literal fulfilment of such imagery.

The final judgment is mentioned, so the watchfulness theme comes in; holiness and goodness may even speed the outcome. 'The new heavens and new earth' again expresses the final fulfilment of the divine promises, which the gift of peace already anticipates.

THIRD READING (MARK 1:1-8)
Make his paths straight

Mark 1:1-8 raises the curtain; these verses are Mark's equivalent of Matthew's and Luke's infancy narratives and John's prologue. Jesus is identified without any doubt as Messiah and Son of God.

John the Baptist is introduced to set the scene. Historically the Baptist has a definite mission. He upbraided the national apostasy by calling all the people to the waters of purification and repentance. John was essentially a lone prophet, working in the spirit of Elijah, the 9th century BC prophet, due to return to prepare for God's definitive entry among his people.

Mark sees John the Baptist exclusively in his role as forerunner to the Mighty One, the Messiah. The prophetic text he quotes brings out John's task as precursor. His clothing, like his baptism, points to the Messiah. A Jewish hope looked to God to tear open the heavens by pouring out his Spirit over his people. John the Baptist prepares for this event by pouring water over the repentant sinner. But the one who will pour out the Spirit is now at hand.

The scripture readings point to the theme of preparation. This can be the personal preparation in holiness of life. But it can also be the preparation of the world for Christ. Anxious questions are asked about current trends, about the place of man in the universe, his role in his nation, his own individual worth. Christians can prepare men to see the answer to their most basic and searching questions in the Good News of Christ.

For a second week the Gospel recalls the witness of John the Baptist to Jesus as the Chosen One of God.

Like the joy of our Lady as she praises God for his graciousness towards her, the later Isaian prophet rejoices because God has given Jerusalem such a glorious salvation. So, too, Christians must be happy and give thanks to God constantly.

This Sunday thus retains the theme of joy it had in the previous missal, where it was termed 'Gaudete Sunday'.

FIRST READING (ISAIAH 61:1-2. 10-11)
I exult for joy in the Lord

Jerusalem, in the mouth of the prophet, rejoices in the gifts of salvation that clothe her and spring up from her to fill the earth.

So close is this passage to the message of the Servant Songs of Second Isaiah, that some feel it to be the fifth of these songs. Others see it as the vocation of a post-exilic Isaian prophet. However, in style and intention it fits in best with the Songs of the First Return from Exile (Isaiah 60–62). Jerusalem is the heroine of these songs: salvation dawns, days of darkness are over, the rebuilding begins and her glory shines out. The prophet is set to preach the good tidings to the poor and broken-hearted. Each word represents a chapter in biblical history. The Spirit is the sign of the messianic era; the anointing is for the prophetic office of proclaiming rescue and complete freedom for God's people. The jubilee year is not just the fiftieth year, but a messianic jubilee that will never end. In St Luke's Gospel, Jesus begins his public preaching by reading the words of this prophecy.

THE RESPONSORIAL PSALM: The final verses of the Reading inspire our Lady's *Magnificat*. The ones who will receive God's blessings are the poor and the lowly who recognize their need when all else has failed.

SECOND READING (THESSALONIANS 5:16-24)
May you all be kept safe, spirit, soul and body, for the coming of the Lord

With words like these Paul expresses his final greetings at the end of his First Letter to the Thessalonians.

Paul has been asked: What about Christians who have already died before the Lord has returned? They will be at no disadvantage, he replied. Paul himself expects to be alive when the Lord returns. Yet he insists on watchfulness.

The Christian life is not a list of do's and dont's. It should be a life of joy, prayer and thanksgiving to God. Most important, Christians must respect the extraordinary gifts that accompany the outpouring of the Spirit of Christ upon the faithful. Obviously they must check that these gifts are good for the community. God is going to be faithful to his promises. He will keep intact and bring to completion the salvation of the body as well as the higher and lower powers of the human spirit. Notice that Jewish thought had no set formula for the divisions of the human personality. There is no need to see 'spirit' here as 'grace', or spell it with a capital letter to mean the Holy Spirit.

THIRD READING (JOHN 1:6-8. 19-28)
There stands among you—unknown to you—the one who is coming after me

These words get to the heart of John's theology. The glorified Jesus is still *present* to his Church, though working unseen in her sacraments.

So important to John is the *witness* to Jesus that is to instil faith. John introduces the Baptist very abruptly as if his readers knew the story already; he is showing them that John the Baptist's true mission was really to bear witness to Jesus, rather than to proclaim a baptism of repentance. John is not the Messiah, nor the Elijah figure intended to precede the Messiah, nor the Prophet like Moses. But who is? John says nothing, but in doing so points implicitly to Jesus.

The evangelist seems to do all he can to demote the Baptist. He is only a voice. His status is only as a slave in the face of the Coming One. The distinction between John's 'I am not' and the 'I am' phrases of Jesus shows more clearly than anything else how the Baptist's figure melts before the person of the Word made flesh, the true light of the world.

The themes of this Mass are contrasting ones. On the one hand, joy and thanksgiving—the Spirit is already poured out, the Good News has been preached, salvation has been assured; the Christian mission is to give thanksgiving for salvation itself and not just for personal redemption. On the other hand, the Gospel makes us question more deeply, Who is he that is to come?

39

FOURTH SUNDAY OF ADVENT   *21 December 1969*

By the Fourth Sunday of Advent the mood of the Liturgy shows that Christmas is at hand. What will the Christ be like?

There is irony in the choice of the First Reading. The Church picks one of the greatest Old Testament passages, yet the text fails to be even a shadow of the reality she preaches. The angel's proclamation to Mary only heightens the contrast. And Paul is lost for words as he attempts to praise the wisdom of God at the end of the Epistle to the Romans.

FIRST READING (2 SAMUEL 7:1-5. 8:11-16)

The kingdom of David will always stand secure before the Lord

Even the writer of the Books of Samuel, remembering the words of this Reading centuries later, knew they had never really been lived up to by any of David's sons. Yet he is still inspired by the divine promise that the dynasty of David would continue for ever. These words originate the stream of prophecies that the Messiah would be a Davidic king. The promise is made personally to David, but it will bring all God's people the pre-eminent divine gifts of peace and security. The prophecy is beautifully constructed around the contrast between the intention of David to build a house for God (the Temple), and the intention of God to build a house for David (his Dynasty).

THE RESPONSORIAL PSALM gives the royal psalmist's reflexion on the Nathan prophecy to David. In this promise of an eternal dynasty, God shows his special and eternal devotion to his people.

SECOND READING (ROMANS 16:25-27)

The mystery, which was kept secret for endless ages, is now made clear

The text of Romans 16:25-27 is thought by some to be an additional liturgical ending to Paul's masterpiece. Paul has made known the Good News in his preaching about Jesus—it is the power of God to root the Romans in its message and ensure they lead their lives true to Christ. But now he sees the Good News as the mystery of God's plan now revealed. God commanded the Good News of Christ to be preached not just so that men might hear about him, but so that they would accept Christ's saving work by personal commitment and submission. So God's providence is extolled, for he has arranged everything so magnificently. All men will be united by being joined to Christ, who alone is the means of giving God proper worship. The mystery is not a mere blueprint of God, but Christ himself, hidden in centuries of preparation, but now held out to the world.

THIRD READING (LUKE 1:26-38)
Listen! You are to conceive and bear a Son

The most important as well as the most hidden of all the figures who prepare for Christ is our Lady herself. In the infancy narrative of Luke, Mary is surrounded by Old Testament shadows. The people of Israel are gathered around her and in her. The salutation to Mary—Miryam, the 'exalted one'—is probably the most striking in the whole Bible. Almost every word has messianic intensity. God is with Mary already, 'gracing' her for the task she is to fulfil. As she is troubled, the salutation is repeated and it is explained that she is to be the mother of the true Davidic king, God's Messiah. How? By the overshadowing of the spirit of God, similar to the way God overshadows his Temple. God's presence would be so powerfully active in her that her child will have all the divine glory as befits his Son. Mary's humble submission in faith and trust gives God's Word scope to take effect in her.

Luke has shown, firstly, that God is going to dwell among his people as their redeemer. Secondly, he reveals the virginity of the instrument chosen to bring this about. Mary may have been reminded of Isaiah 7:14: 'The maiden is with child and will soon give birth to a son.' She may have seen that her sublime office was better carried out by continuing her virginal state.

Did Mary know her son was God? It is likely that she realized that God was more than ever before present in her son; her son's life and mission would be the direct intervention of God himself. Remember it took the Church three centuries to make the formal and official assent to Christ's divinity (Nicea 325).

In answer to the question 'What will Christ be like?', two trends emerge from the Readings: Christ is the Royal Messiah with an eternal rule—Christ is a mysterious divine person, who came not to deny the world, but to show concern for it and save it.

41

THE SEASON OF CHRISTMAS

The Season of Christmas is centred around the commemoration of Christ's nativity, and his manifestation, firstly to the Jewish people (symbolized in the shepherds), and secondly to the nations (symbolized in the visit of the Magi).

It is the second most important season of the liturgical year; the paschal mysteries, which include Pentecost, being the first. Christmas has a Vigil Mass and retains its octave. It is still permitted to celebrate three Masses on Christmas Day.

The previous Christmas cycle of feasts has been reorganized in the new Calendar:

The First Sunday after Christmas is now the Feast of the Holy Family.

New Year's Day, the Octave Day of Christmas, incorporates the Circumcision and the Holy Name into the restored ancient Feast of Mary Mother of God.

The Second Sunday after Christmas remembers especially the Biblical Theology of the Incarnation.

The Epiphany[1] stresses the call of the pagans to faith in Christ.

The Sunday after the Epiphany is now the Feast of the Baptism of our Lord.

In the Lectionary the tendency is to retain traditional Christmas readings, especially in the Masses of Christmas itself. As one might expect, the Christmas Feasts have enough biblical foundation to attract those passages which recall their origin.

The special Vigil Mass of Christmas considers the lineage of Jesus, especially in the Second and Third Readings.

Isaian messianic prophecies accompany the readings traditional in the Christmas Masses.

On the Feast of the Holy Family, the first two readings consider morality in the home, while the Gospel recalls the presentation in the Temple and the early growth of Jesus.

On the Motherhood of our Lady, the Gospel repeats the Dawn Gospel of Christmas, adding the verse about the naming of Jesus.

The passage of Isaiah that inspires so many of the traditions

---

[1] If the Epiphany is not a Holy Day of Obligation, it is transferred from 6 January to 4 January 1970, and in future years to the Sunday falling between 2 and 8 January. It thus replaces the Second Sunday after Christmas.

surrounding the Epiphany becomes the First Reading of the Feast.

The Feast of the Baptism underlines the Mission of Jesus by having one of Isaiah's Servant Songs in the First Reading.

The purpose of the Christmas liturgy is to remind us of the incarnation. All the feasts revolve around this fundamental theme. It is the story of God's condescension and love. His Son submits to our condition. Again and again the fact is brought home that he took a human nature like ours. It was not pretence, for it was God's way of making us his children—sons in the Son. The Feasts of the Christmas cycle are so many pictures of this one world-shaking happening—Christ became one of us.

The evangelist John crystallizes this theme into few words:

> The Word was made flesh,
> he lived among us,
> and we saw his glory,
> the glory that is his as the only Son of the Father
> full of grace and truth (John 1:14).

A special Vigil Mass may be said in the evening of 24 December. This Mass opens the liturgical season of Christmas.

After the praise of the new Jerusalem in the reading from Isaiah, the theme is concentrated on the lineage of Jesus. The Second Reading pinpoints David and John the Baptist as heralds of the Saviour, while the Gospel gives the pedigree of Christ from Abraham to Joseph. If only two readings are to be used, it would be best to omit the First in order to preserve unity of theme.

FIRST READING (ISAIAH 62:1-5)
The Lord takes delight in you

This Reading is again taken from the Songs of the Return from Exile, Isaiah 60–62. The prophet breaks into praise of the new Jerusalem, as he waits for God's splendour to shine out from her. She will be a silent ruin no longer. The days of sterility and bereavement are over. As she begins to live again, she becomes the symbol of God's faithful devotion to his people and the sign of universal salvation. A new name is given her; not 'Forsaken' or 'Abandoned' one, but God's 'Delight'. The land is proud and prosperous because of her. The prophet does not mention past adulteries. He sees this as her first marriage to her God.

Closely linked with the glories of Jerusalem is the promise made to the House of David from which her kings come.

THE RESPONSORIAL PSALM sings of this promise. Endowed with divine sonship, her kings become the greatest on earth and protect her as a shield.

SECOND READING (ACTS 13:16-17. 22-25)
Paul's witness to Christ, the son of David

It was constant practice in the early missions of the Church to evangelize first the Jewish Synagogue. This first recorded sermon of Paul is very much in the pattern of previous sermons in Acts, especially that of Stephen before he was stoned (chapter 7).

Paul enumerates the great blessings of God for his people, the choice of Abraham, the Exodus from Egypt, the entry into the promised land. Then (omitting mention of the Judges and Saul) he recalls God's promise to David and jumps immediately to Jesus who alone really fulfils this promise. In Paul's Letters there is no mention of John the Baptist. It looks as if Luke is putting a favourite theme of his own in the mouth of Paul—the very close connection of John the Baptist's mission with our Lord. For Luke, John is already a New Testament figure, preparing the people to recognize the need for salvation. In few but striking words, this Reading marshals the whole sweep of God's plan of salvation.

THIRD READING (MATTHEW 1:1-25)
The Genealogy of Jesus Christ, Son of David

Matthew and Luke are the evangelists who list for us the ancestors of Jesus. As these two insist so much on the continuity between the old and new people of God, one expects them to underline the solidarity of Jesus with his people.

Matthew, especially, marks the true Israel as the people who accept Jesus as their Lord. It is very important for him to link Jesus with Abraham. He is the seal of the promise made to the founder of the old chosen people. Matthew also points to Jesus as the fulfilment of the promise of an eternal dynasty made to David. Jesus' Davidic lineage comes through Joseph, who remains the central figure throughout Matthew's infancy narrative (rather than Mary).

We know the genealogies of lineage were very important to Jewish families ever since the Exile, to prove purity of blood. Perhaps Matthew had access to memorized lists. However, the artificial nature of his list is obvious. Three sets of fourteen names, with a new series beginning at David and the Babylonian exile, show considerable schematization. Some suggest that Mary makes up number 14 of the third series to stress the virgin birth.

The abbreviated Reading concentrates on the last eight verses. This is Matthew's account of Jesus' birth. The divine plan is communicated to Joseph rather than Mary. The child who will bear his name brings to fulfilment the prophetic promise that God dwells with his people through the Davidic Messiah.

Because God took a long time in preparing for his salvation, it does not mean that he abandoned his people. In this Mass we see the theme of the divine condescension, so much a characteristic of the Feast of the Incarnation. God entrusts his plan to human hands and human decision. Christ is hailed as the expected of the nations. His Gospel proves itself a leaven of liberty and progress and brings about a brotherhood of unity and peace.

Three sets of Readings are given for the Christmas Masses, following the precedent of the previous Missal. Most of the passages are the traditional Christmas ones. The celebrant may select from these three Masses the most suitable readings for his congregation. It may be wise to read the Prologue of St John in Masses celebrated after the early morning in accordance with the previous practice.

The Night Mass is the Mass of Christ's Birth. The time has come, says the Gospel. The greatest of Isaiah's messianic prophecies explains what this means. For Paul, this event gives the basic support to all our moral effort.

FIRST READING (ISAIAH 9:1-7)
A Son is given to us

In this passage, taken from Isaiah's Book of Immanuel (chapters 6–12), the contours of Israel's messianic hope are startlingly vivid. It may be best to see this oracle against the background of court protocol. At the enthronement of a new king, the characteristics of his religious and royal ancestors are given as ceremonial titles. His coronation day makes the new king a hero, adopted as God's own son. He has the wisdom of Solomon, the courage of David, the outstanding virtues of the patriarchs, Moses and the prophets. But more important he is a new fulfilment of God's promise to David. No longer will the people be led off under the yokes of captivity. The new child will end all that. Isaiah looks beyond the possibilities of any king of his time, to the Ideal King, the new David. God's jealousy—his zeal to fulfil what he has promised, not his punishing anger—is going to give his people this ideal king.

THE RESPONSORIAL PSALM takes up the mood of joy with a Hymn of Praise to God, king of all the nations, judge who is faithful to his promises.

SECOND READING (TITUS 2:11-14)
God's grace has been revealed to the whole human race

God's universal blessing has come and is now made known to us, says Paul. Christ has set us free and made us his people, the kind of people 'zealous' for good deeds because we are still hoping for the complete outcome of a salvation that is no mere gazing at the past, but a future appearance and presence of our divine Lord. This text is a rare example of Paul confessing Christ's divinity in unambiguous terms; he is attacking pagan 'gods' and 'saviours' who can never really help us.

THIRD READING (LUKE 2:1-14)
Today a Saviour has been born to you

The words of the angel to the shepherds crystallize the meaning of this feast.

'The time came . . .', says Luke. Centuries of hanging onto the divine promise have ended. In a hymnic, meditative style, Luke, the theologian of salvation history, telescopes all Israel's past into his narratives of the infancy. The great men of the past cast their shadow on his story which is essentially a message of redemption. Over Bethlehem stands her greatest son, David. He witnesses God's promise to him coming to pass, not only for his own people, but for the blessing of the whole world.

The sixth century AD computation by Denis the Small was mistaken in taking Luke's thirty years (3:23) too literally. Jesus would probably have been born about 6 BC. The census that causes Joseph to return to his ancestral home was no doubt for taxation purposes. The outer part of the cave (closed over with wood, the 'inn') was not private enough, so Joseph took Mary back into the cave where the animals were stabled.

Shepherds were far from romantic characters; they were lonely social misfits of doubted honesty. But God, the true Shepherd of Israel, intended his message for all social classes of men. The glory of God is over the Bethlehem field and over a tiny child, as of old it was over the Temple. The time of fear has ended, the time of joy begun. To the men of God's choice, who have received his message and accepted his Son, comes the new era of messianic peace.

The spirit of this Mass is to be found in a joy that expresses amazement of what God has done. We may not have realized fully that this world can never be the same place any more after the birth of Christ has happened. From the moment of his birth, God's Son showed us what being a successful man means. His was a submissive attitude that brings about human brotherhood not through power but through peace.

CHRISTMAS: DAWN MASS   25 *December 1969*

The focus of the Night Mass has been on the birth of the Saviour. We have seen his glory and his humility. Now the Liturgy turns the cameras towards the effects of this birth on us.

In the Gospel, the shepherds break out into praise of God because of what they have experienced. In the mouth of Isaiah: Victory has been achieved. We are now God's people. For Paul the appearance of Christ is a completely free gift, which not only achieves a new birth, but also gives us a right to possess the same sort of eternal life that Christ possesses.

FIRST READING (ISAIAH 62:11-12)
Look, your saviour comes

The verses of the First Reading conclude the Songs of the Return from Exile (Isaiah 60–62), so often used in the Advent Liturgy. The waiting has finished. The final phrases of these songs of joy can be proclaimed. The road for the return has been built; it is sound, swept clean and signposted; the whole world re-echoes God's edict for Jerusalem, 'Look, your saviour comes'. In victorious procession, the saviour comes to renew his people. Jerusalem receives back the presence of God. More than just a road to bring the exiles back, God's highway to Jerusalem is a Way of Pilgrimage for all the nations of the earth.

RESPONSORIAL PSALM: another traditional Christmas Psalm is used. God, King and Judge, is coming as Master of the whole earth.

SECOND READING (TITUS 3:4-7)
It was for no reason except his own compassion that he saved us

In terms of great beauty, Paul tells of the change brought about by Christ. The passage is a mini-anthology of so many of Paul's themes. The Pastoral Epistles (I-II Timothy and Titus) are characterized by the alternation of special instructions and condemnations of false doctrines. But occasionally Paul lets himself go in flights of doctrinal ecstasy. Both God, the Father, and Jesus are called our 'Saviour', a term he never before used. The kindness and love of God stresses the terms so often applied to God in the Old Testament. His fidelity and guidance throughout the

48

centuries was solicitous for our salvation even when we seemed not to want it. But now God has made known that salvation has been achieved. To the man of faith comes Baptism, and the gifts of the Holy Spirit, the seal of our eternal life. Succinctly Paul recalls his teaching about faith that he explained in the Epistle to the Romans (especially in chapter 8).

THIRD READING (LUKE 2:15-20)
The shepherds found Mary and Joseph and the baby

The Dawn Mass continues the Gospel of Midnight Mass. The Shepherds react as Mary did to her angelic visitation—'with haste'. She and they were both given signs of what was happening; Mary was given the sign of Elizabeth's *son*; the shepherds were directed towards the newborn child that was to signify the presence of the Lord among his people, as Saviour and Messiah. 'With haste' is how the poor and outcast react to the preaching of Christ during his public life. Being without hope, they receive someone to hope in. The shepherds glorify and praise God for what they had witnessed, a typical reaction to divine interventions in Old Testament times, and for that reason frequent in Luke.

Mary pondered these things in her heart, the way Jacob felt about Joseph's dreams (Genesis 37:11), and Daniel about his vision of the Son of Man at the Throne of God (Daniel 7:27). Faced with the mysteries of God, she did not really understand.

The Mass is about our reaction to the appearance of the Saviour. We can take the cue from Mary and ponder these things. The meditative part of Christian life is not wasting time. It leads us to stop and think. We need to do this if it is going to sink in that God really can do this sort of thing. God does not stop being God because his Son submits to our ways.

The Liturgy of Christmas holds back the force of what has happened until the Day Mass. Then it hits us: God has acted. It is not promise, it is fact; and hence the world has to change.

God has shown us his arm, says Isaiah. He has finished with spreading his word among many men of different periods and spoken to us in his Son. The incomprehensible theme of Christmas comes out at last—'the Word was made flesh and lived among us'.

First Reading (Isaiah 52:7-10)
All the ends of the earth shall see the salvation of our God

This Reading forms the climax to a long poem of Second Isaiah (Isaiah 51–52). The prophet sings a hymn to God, and a praise of the Jerusalem which now receives the good news of God's Salvation. She has no human king. God himself is now her king and will spread his reign among the nations. The messenger is seen running along the mountain ridges to the Holy City with the news of the exiles' return; the watchman takes it up and proclaims it to the ruined Zion. Now Yahweh returns to his city and is enthroned over her.

Responsorial Psalm: very much in the spirit of Second Isaiah, a hymn of God's new victories is sung. All the nations feel God's 'arm' and experience his justice and salvation.

Second Reading (Hebrews 1:1-6)
God has spoken to us through his Son

Throughout the Old Testament, God revealed the plan of redemption in this way or that to the forerunners and ancestors of the Christian faith. But now the 'end time' has come. God has revealed and achieved all he promised through his Son.

Hebrews is very much an Epistle of Fulfilment. The author focuses, now on the glory of the Son, now on the humiliation he had to suffer to gain it. God's final total word is preached to those in danger of falling away from it.

In a Christmas Mass it is more important to see the Son as pre-existent, different and more excellent than the angels. He was co-founder of the universe with God. His Sonship was not adoptive as it was in David and his successors. He can be compared with a mirror reflecting back God's own image.

In the mind of the author the incarnation is the first stage in

50

the acceptance of our human condition. This acceptance demanded of Jesus the deepest self-identification with men, and issues in the highest gift of glory.

Third Reading (John 1:1-18)
The Word was made flesh and lived among us

The Prologue of St John is the traditional Gospel of Christmas Day. John seems to express better than anyone else the deepest meaning of this mystery. The Prologue may be an early Christian hymn. If it is, John adapts it to be his own special account of our Lord's birth.

The Word shares the Father's divine being and his creative activity. Through him comes the communication and revelation of true and eternal life. But even when faced with the testimony of the Word himself, the world and God's own people would not cross the threshold of faith. Human enterprise could never be responsible for this faith, just as it could never be responsible for the incarnation of God's Word. As of old God dwelt in the Covenant Tent, and in his Temple, so now in a more wondrous way he dwells among those who did receive him. The Incarnate Word brought men face to face with God, not in the magnificence of divine cosmic power, but in witness, faith and love, the personal touch of the man, Jesus of Nazareth. It was in him that 'grace and truth', the faithful devotion with which God honoured his Old Testament covenant, is again made visible. So the divine presence, 'the glory of God', is experienced in the Church, in a superabundance of divine favour that overshadows so completely the old covenant made with Moses. The Church listens in faith to the revelation of him who alone can make God known.

To use the Gospel of John at all immediately brings up the theme of faith. We have heard about the characteristics of the Saviour who brought God to man. We can speculate about the pre-existence of God's Son. But we have to come down to basic matters. A good many people have not received Christ and don't even want to accept him. A community of human beings has accepted him and continues to do so. The secret? If we can call it a secret, it is faith. Centred in this faith is the conviction that when we preach Christ properly, God will not refuse his Holy Spirit to those who genuinely want him.

51

FIRST SUNDAY AFTER CHRISTMAS, THE FEAST OF THE HOLY FAMILY
28 December 1969

This Mass recalls at once the infancy of Jesus (in the Gospel) and the inspiration left us by the Holy Family at Nazareth.

The first two readings talk about conduct in the home. Respect for parents is one of the marks of the wise man. Love and respect for others are the characteristics of the Christian home. The Gospel describes the presentation of Jesus in the Temple and his early growth at Nazareth.

FIRST READING (ECCLESIASTICUS 3:2-6. 12-14)
He who fears the Lord respects his parents

Beginning his work about 180 BC, Ben Sirach's (Ecclesiasticus') purpose is to praise wisdom. 'The fear of the Lord is the beginning of wisdom' (1:14); fear in this text means reverence and obedience. Especially important in the growth of wisdom is patience and confidence in God; but high on the list of virtues that cluster around wisdom is the respect paid to one's parents. Today's First Reading sums up Ben Sirach's passage on honouring one's parents, which is probably a commentary on the Fourth Commandment : 'Honour your father and your mother that your days may be long in the land which the Lord your God gives you' (Exodus 20:12). Important for this feast, the reparation for one's sins can come from respect towards one's father.

THE RESPONSORIAL PSALM is taken from one of the Wisdom Psalms, extolling the acknowledgement and obedience to God that is true fear of him. Such 'fear' will bring benefits to the family —prosperity and many children.

SECOND READING (COLOSSIANS 3:12-21)
Family life in the Lord

Only the last few verses of this Reading are directed towards the family. But the attitudes of the Christian recommended in the first part of the Reading obviously apply to the home.

Colossians is a letter very much centred on the person of Christ. So Paul in his application of doctrine to conduct stresses Christ as model. 'Christ is all and in all' (3:11). He showed us a love which flows over and binds together all other attitudes. A life directed by this love extends the peace of Christ into the whole community. It promotes mutual understanding and genuine Christian wisdom. Christ continues his life of praise and thanksgiving to his Father in the members of his community.

Paul wants the home to be a special example of this. He gives a section on family morality, listing exhortations for the members of the *familia* (which includes the slaves of the household too). Love and harmony are the marks of the Christian home.

THIRD READING (LUKE 2:22-40)
The child grew, filled with wisdom

Wisdom has been mentioned in both readings so far. In Jesus too it brings closeness to God, the sign of real maturity.

Ever since David captured Jerusalem from its Canaanite inhabitants (about 1000 BC), it became the symbol of God's reign among his people. Of all the places on earth, Jerusalem was privileged to feel the intimate presence of God, which they termed his 'glory'. Luke is very much aware of this history. He pushes it before our minds, as the infant Jesus is brought with Mary and Joseph to the Holy City. The Child has to be 'bought back', because as the first-born son he belongs to God. There is irony here. Luke knows that Jesus belonged entirely to God from his very conception. Yet the Holy Family belongs to the chosen people; the Law of Moses must be carried out on this occasion —as Jesus did throughout his life.

Luke does not mention the Magi or the Flight into Egypt. Nazareth was the home of Mary and Joseph and there they returned. Luke indicates that Jesus grew up in physical strength and stature, and stresses his growth in wisdom. He links wisdom with God's favour, so underlining the development of Jesus' human consciousness of his own unique relationship with his Father. Through Jesus' continual contact with the heavenly Father, the Holy Family grew in that dedication to God that is the pattern for all Christian families.

Example teaches best. This is constantly stressed as the motto of the Christian home. Love, harmony and mutual respect have to be taught in action. The Spirit of Christ is present in the home because he dwells in the hearts of its members. But what of those without homes, who have not the means of leading a truly human family life, without food, clothing and shelter? This is an area of true Christian love and concern.

THE OCTAVE OF CHRISTMAS AND FEAST OF MARY, MOTHER OF GOD

New Year's Day, the Octave Day of Christmas, celebrates the restored Feast of our Lady's Motherhood. It also commemorates the giving of the Holy Name to Jesus. The Feast of the Holy Name is no longer in the Church's Calendar.

The Gospel recalls both themes of the day, whilst the First Reading tells what blessings come from the invocation of God's name on his people, and the Second underlines the fact of Christ's birth from a woman and his subjection to God's old Law.

FIRST READING (NUMBERS 6:22-27)

They are to call down my name on the sons of Israel and I will bless them

In the Book of Numbers is found the beautiful priestly blessing made over the people after the morning sacrifice. So sacred was this prayer, that the divine name YAHWEH was used, instead of LORD or 'my Lord', that replaced the divine name in the synagogue service. The petition was intensified as the triple blessing progressed. The priest prayed for the preservation of the people, then for the prosperity of all under God's gaze and favour; finally God's complete blessing is invoked—peace : the sum total of all they could desire. This peace enters the world at Jesus' birth.

As the RESPONSORIAL PSALM repeats phrases of the blessing, it begs God to fulfil it and thanks him for the way he has done so already. The whole world is touched by the blessing of Israel.

SECOND READING (GALATIANS 4:4-7)

God sent his Son, born of a woman

Today's feast points to the Mother of Jesus. Paul explains the birth of Jesus from Mary as part and parcel of the human condition he adopted.

So often in his life Paul had to defend his preaching in the face of opposing doctrines. Galatians explains the dogma that is so classical in Paul : God's salvation comes as a free gift to the men who accept the Gospel in faith. He argues his case in intricate fashion around the figure of Abraham. But what is probably the real kernel of the Letter is found in today's Second Reading.

In the ancient household, even the son and heir had to submit

54

to the slave appointed as pedagogue during his minority. The Old Testament Law demanded our submission as if we were slaves. Even God's Son accepted human birth and the condition of slavery under this Law. But this Son's mission was to make us grow up, to redeem us from this slavery to the Law and make us full sons in God's household. We know this has happened because the Spirit of God has been sent by the Son into our hearts, making us God's adopted sons. With his natural Son, we can address God in the most intimate of ways—'Abba, Father'. Though we are now free of slavery we still have to wait for the complete outcome, our final redemption and resurrection.

Mary's position as Jesus' mother is to share in all his work. So she becomes the Mother of the Church, his body on earth.

THIRD READING (LUKE 2:16-21)
They found Mary and Joseph and the baby . . . When the eighth day came, they gave him the name Jesus

This Reading repeats the Gospel of Christmas Dawn, adding verse 21, about the circumcision and naming of Jesus.

Just as John the Baptist's name and mission were confirmed when he was circumcised, so it was with Jesus. Jesus' mission was expressed in his name, Yeshua, 'salvation' or in the popular mind 'God saves'. This was a common name; but the fact that it was given before his conception, shows God's intention that the name should express what his life and work should be.

Circumcision united Jesus to the chosen people. It made him an heir to the promises to Abraham—promises fulfilled in Jesus.

Mary has a unique relationship with her Son; she must have understood him in a special way. Her salvation came through the faith and trust she showed in the actual bearing of her child. All her privileges stem from this divine motherhood.

This feast is a combination of many themes—Jesus' birth of a human mother, the mission of our Lady, the circumcision and naming of Jesus.

Once again the liturgy is trying to hammer home God's acceptance of our condition. But in his turn his Son is the sign and sacrament of the oneness of all mankind. The Body of Christ, his Church, has our Lady as its mother. She symbolizes the unity of heart and mind that the members of Christ's body are meant to show to others.

SECOND SUNDAY AFTER CHRISTMAS *4 January 1970*

The Mass of the newly titled Second Sunday after Christmas returns to the basic theme of the Christmas mystery, so vividly portrayed in the Day Mass of 25 December—the Incarnation.

The Prologue of John is repeated. The other readings highlight, more than the Christmas Mass does, the pre-existence of Christ, through the themes of Wisdom personified and God's eternal election.

FIRST READING (ECCLESIASTICUS 24:1-2. 8-12)
The Wisdom of God has pitched her tent among the chosen people

The evangelist John finds in the chapter of Ben Sirach used in this reading, a way to express who Jesus really was.

Chapter 24 is not just the centre of Ben Sirach's book as far as arrangement is concerned. He reaches in it a climax in his praise of wisdom. The Wisdom of God dwells among his chosen people. Wisdom is almost personified; she originates in God and was present with him in the creation of the universe. Ben Sirach goes even further. Wisdom is identified with the Law of Moses, thus giving the religion of Israel a place in the creation itself. Like the waters of the earth, wisdom will flood and irrigate all nations and all generations.

God's transcendence was very vivid to the sages of Israel. The presence of wisdom was their way of expressing God's nearness to the people. Wisdom was consequently linked with other expressions of God's contact with his people, his Word and his Shekinah ('Presence'). St John could so easily use these terms to express the kind of way God became present to men in the Incarnation of his Son.

THE RESPONSORIAL PSALM praises the Word of God which has such marvellous effects as it visits the earth. This word which so powerfully and providently forms the earth, forms and restores Israel.

SECOND READING (EPHESIANS 1:3-6. 15-18)
He determined that we should become his adopted sons through Jesus

St Paul's Benediction of God beginning his Epistle to the

Ephesians is one of the theological highpoints of the New Testament. As in the Old Testament hymns, God is blessed, and his works that so deserve this blessing are recounted (1:3-14). The whole Trinity is involved in the divine plan for men. From his throne of majesty, the Father chooses us in his Son. 'In Christ' and 'in him' occur very frequently in the Letter. The blessings which flow from this choice come to us in the Holy Spirit. To have the blessing of an eternal communion with God is none other than the sharing in the life which belongs properly to God's beloved Son. In this hymn is found the clearest statement of the recapituation of all things in Christ (1:10).

Such is God's eternal plan. The Ephesians' reputation in faith and love reminds Paul of God's secret now revealed in Christ. The Church becomes absorbed in God and is convinced of his blessing still to be completed.

THIRD READING (JOHN 1:1-18)

The Word was made flesh, and lived among us

John sees in Jesus the real subject of God's cosmic purpose. Ben Sirach showed that the just man becomes God's son through obedience to the Law, the Law which is the embodiment of God's wisdom, present at the creation of the world. Likewise, John sees God's Word as present at the creation. This Word becomes flesh, the life and light of the world to those who accept him as God's true revelation. Jesus is the new embodiment of God's Wisdom that replaces the Law of Moses.

Like Paul, John insists on the grace and truth needed to see what God is doing in Jesus and to grasp what he is doing for us.

The biblical theology of the incarnation is paramount in this Mass. This will not make it easy to preach about. The theme of wisdom can help us to see the unity of creation. The incarnation did not cut across human needs. Jesus took our human condition upon himself; he too had to grow up a wise and prudent human being. In our day wisdom and intelligence are needed even more if we are to humanize the countless new discoveries on our hands. God's wisdom does not strip our own. It only shows us up when we become foolish.

57

THE EPIPHANY   *6 January 1970*

The Feast of the Epiphany commemorates the call of the nations to salvation.

No one is more suitable to proclaim the universal mission of Christ than the Apostle of the Gentiles, Paul; Isaiah has seen God making Jerusalem the light which attracts all the nations. And the Gospel story of the Magi symbolizes the manifestation of the incarnate Son to all the peoples of the earth.

FIRST READING (ISAIAH 60:1-6)
Above you the glory of the Lord appears

Right from the first words, the double imperative, 'Arise, shine', we see the influence of Second Isaiah on the Songs of the Return from Exile (Isaiah 60–62). What Second Isaiah hoped for is now coming true.

In two images the prophet expresses God's presence: the brightness that lights up the Holy City like a beacon, and the dark cloud that surrounds the place where he makes his will known. Both of these were present in the Exodus, when Yahweh formed his people from the slaves of Egypt and himself led them into the land he had promised. But much more important for the feast of the Epiphany, the universal dimension is everywhere visible in the text. Nations and kings will come to Jerusalem and look to her for guidance. They pour their riches into her in recognition of her God and King. This passage has inspired much of the popular devotion surrounding the feast of the Epiphany, when Jesus becomes the star shining to the nations afar.

The prophet is much influenced by the Royal Psalm used as RESPONSORIAL PSALM. The king (Solomon?) rules world-wide in justice and peace. He receives the tribute of the nations in precious gifts, yet is the protector of the poor and the weak, their redeemer from oppression.

SECOND READING (EPHESIANS 3:2-3. 5-6)
It has now been revealed that pagans share the same inheritance

A second time in Ephesians Paul is praising the majesty of God's plan, so mysterious until Christ reveals it to those who believe in him. In a nutshell: God plans that through Christ the

58

pagans are called to have a part with the Jews in his new people, the body of Christ.

From his first calling (Paul never calls it a conversion) on the road to Damascus, it was specially revealed to him that this was God's plan for the nations, and that he was to be their apostle. Not even in Isaiah was it known of old that it was God's intention to break down the dividing wall between Jew and non-Jew. Now all men are to be co-heirs, co-members and co-sharers in a body with Christ as its head. Paul is here giving his best explanation of this mystery; his understanding of it was one of the greatest dynamos of his missionary life.

THIRD READING (MATTHEW 2:1-12)

We saw his star and have come to do the king homage

The only words we hear on the lips of the Magi are: 'Where is the infant king of the Jews? We saw his star in the east and have come to do him homage.'

Crossweaving of themes by Matthew makes interpretation difficult. The Jews take little interest in Jesus, and Herod has only hatred. It is people from afar that come to worship. The quotation of Micah 5:1-3 (reflecting the invitation offered to David to become king of all Israel) is used to draw attention to the Davidic Messiahship of the child. The gifts may point to the divinity of this tiny baby, though Matthew is quite obviously relying heavily on the passage of Isaiah read at this Mass.

The naming of the three 'kings', Kaspar (= Moor), Balthasar and Melchior, and the symbolism of the gifts are traditions that took fourteen centuries to perfect. The Persian word 'Magi' confirms that these visitors were men skilled in things sacred, especially in the worship of astral deities.

There is not much to be gained from discussing the intricacies of this Magi visit. The manifestation of Christ to all men, symbolized in the worship of the Magi, is taken by the Church into the wider mystery of our presence at Christ's incarnation. The three 'Gentiles' include ourselves, those who have learned later to come and worship him. As the Church is present before her incarnate Lord, we are reminded of a divided Christianity, especially the Eastern Churches for whom the Epiphany is the greatest of the Christmas Feasts.

SUNDAY AFTER EPIPHANY. FEAST OF THE
BAPTISM OF OUR LORD   *11 January 1970*

In the new Calendar, the Sunday following the Epiphany is the feast of the Baptism of Jesus, formerly 13 January. Strictly speaking, this is the First Sunday of the Year, but the Mass formula with the theme of Christ's Baptism prevents this Sunday having readings of its own.

Three aspects of the feast appear in the readings: the presence of the Spirit, the calling of Jesus for his mission, and the fact that God was with him and took pleasure in him.

FIRST READING (ISAIAH 42:1-4. 6-7)
Here is my servant in whom my soul delights

'I have endowed him with my Spirit' (Is 42:1) makes the First Song of the Servant of Yahweh an obvious choice for this feast.

In this first Song, the Servant is declared the chosen one on whom God's pleasure rests. Endowed with the Spirit of God, he will bring salvation to the nations; like David's messianic son, he brings true justice and peace; like Moses he will teach men the Law of God; God's Voice goes out to the ends of the earth to present his Servant, who works not with exterior force but within the hearts of all men.

The God who so marvellously created the world is able to form his Servant (from his mother's womb, says the Third Song, Is 49:1) to be a covenant to the people of Israel and 'a light to the nations'. The blindness First Isaiah threatens is swept away.

THE RESPONSORIAL PSALM is extremely old; it envisages a storm sweeping in from the Mediterranean to the eastern desert. It extols God's power over nature. Thunder was thought to be the voice of God speaking from heaven. Hence the psalm is fitting for this feast which celebrates a voice from heaven on the Son.

SECOND READING (ACTS 10:34-38)
God anointed him with the Holy Spirit

The last missionary discourse of Peter in the Acts of the Apostles is meant to typify his preaching to those who are not Jews. The style makes it a very early summary of Church preaching, which the Synoptic Gospels eventually used. Yet for all that, themes typical of Luke characterize the sermon: e.g. the word, meaning the 'good news of peace' that Jesus taught. Especially important for this feast, Jesus' Baptism is described in the terms of 'God anointing Jesus of Nazareth with the Holy Spirit and with power'. All the evangelists insist that the Spirit-directed mission of Jesus began with his Baptism. But Luke underlines much more than the others the close supervision of that mission by the Holy Spirit. Jesus is specially endowed with the Holy Spirit at the beginning of his public life. This Luke calls an 'anointing' —an obvious reflexion on Jesus as the Christ, God's Anointed.

Third Reading (Mark 1:7-11)
You are my Son, the Beloved; my favour rests on you

Though Mark knew that John the Baptist's work was much more extensive than he relates, he casts the Baptist in an essentially preparatory role. After only a few verses, John drops to the background, and the Spirit and Voice of God take over as the actors of the short Baptism scene with Jesus.

Three themes can help the understanding of the text. Firstly, the Father's voice (audible only to Jesus in Mark) uses the words of Psalm 2, which has in mind the adoption as God's Son of a king when he was anointed with his coronation oil. For Jesus this is a royal anointing for his Mission as Messianic King. Secondly, the pleasure in the Son, and the giving of the Spirit, remind us of the Suffering Servant songs in Isaiah and stress the function of Jesus as the Messiah who must suffer—important in the second part of Mark's Gospel. Thirdly, Jesus is for Mark the vicarious representative of all men, especially in his suffering. The Baptism stresses his representative status as the new Israel coming from the waters of a new Exodus, beginning the new age characterized by the opening of heaven and the pouring out of the Spirit on all men.

One can hardly talk about the Baptism of Jesus without thinking of the sacraments of Christian initiation, Baptism and Confirmation. The same kind of themes characterize these sacraments. The pleasure of the Father makes the Christian his son. The anointing of the Spirit brings the man of faith into a close communion with God. But the third thing gives us more to think about: Jesus' Baptism began his mission. So too, Christian Baptism means the mission of the Christian to communicate to the rest of men the blessing he has received.

The Yearly Cycle

Outside the Christmas and Paschal cycles, 33 or 34 Sundays remain, and are termed Sundays 'per annum', or Sundays of the Year.

The Lectionary gives 33 Mass formulae, though not all of these will be used. For the First Sunday 'per annum' is the Feast of the Baptism of Jesus and closes the Christmas cycle, and the Feast of the Blessed Trinity replaces the Sunday after Pentecost, as previously. The last Sunday 'per annum' is now the Feast of Christ the King, but its readings are included in the Sundays 'per annum' lists.

The Sundays 'per annum' begin with Sunday 2, after the Feast of the Baptism—Sunday 2 in 1970 occurs on 18 January. They end with Sunday 5 (8 February) to allow for Lent and Paschaltide, but begin again with Sunday 9 (31 May) and continue till Sunday 34 (22 November). Sundays 6–8 are omitted in 1970, though the Weekday Readings omit only Week 6. The reason for this is that the Octave of Pentecost is now suppressed and Weekday Readings of Week 7 begin on Whit Monday; though Sunday 6 is omitted, Sundays 7 and 8 are replaced by Pentecost and the Blessed Trinity. This kind of arrangement better preserves the eschatological theme of the Second Coming of Christ on the final Sundays 'per annum'.

Sundays 2–5 of Year Two

The semi-continuous reading of Mark's Gospel begins on Sunday 3. The Gospel of Sunday 2 is a passage from John about the call of the disciples which continues the Manifestation theme of the Epiphany.

In the Second Reading, the semi-continuous reading of First Corinthians 6–11 begins on Sunday 2; see the Introduction to First Corinthians above (pp. 25–7).

Old Testament Readings are chosen on the principle that they tie in with the Gospel, in order to show the unity of Old and New Testaments. However, it is the intention of the Lectionary to give a wide selection, so that all the most important passages in the Old Testament are heard at one time or another. Hence texts of four very different books are read on these Sundays:

Sunday 2: First Samuel—The call of Samuel.

Sunday 3: Jonah—Nineveh repents.

Sunday 4: Deuteronomy—The Prophet like Moses.

Sunday 5: Job—The drudgery of man's day.

It is important to note the headings of each reading. The Sundays of the Year are concerned with the mystery of Christ in a great variety of aspects. The headings help to show which aspect is being considered; the Old Testament combines with the Gospel in this respect. The Second Readings tend to be quite independent.

SECOND SUNDAY OF THE YEAR   18 January 1970

The theme of the Mass is the call of God and man's reply to it.

The Gospel gives St John's version of the calling of the disciples, Andrew and John, Peter and James. Samuel too had to recognize God's voice. First Corinthians (beginning the semi-continuous reading of the centre chapters of the Letter) tells how the Christian belongs to Christ, body as well as soul.

FIRST READING (1 SAMUEL 3:3-10. 19)

Speak, Lord, your servant is listening

The Old Testament gives the call of Samuel in detail to stress the importance of this figure in Israel's history. The call of Moses is given with similar attention. Not only was Samuel the last of the warrior-heroes we call the Judges, but he inaugurated the monarchy and began the all-important prophetic movement. This chapter of First Samuel also explains the rejection of the priestly family of Eli, whom Samuel replaces. But as usual in the Books of Samuel-Kings it is his prophetic rather than priestly character that is underlined. God was with him and no word of God went unheeded.

THE RESPONSORIAL PSALM continues the mood of listening to God and obediently proclaiming God's word.

SECOND READING (CORINTHIANS 6:13-15. 17-20)

Your bodies are members making up the body of Christ

Paul is not only having trouble with those members of the Corinthian community who claim to be masters of the Christian message, but also these same people want to solve moral questions in their own fashion. After all, Paul did proclaim Christian freedom from the Law! Isn't the sexual appetite like eating and drinking?

The apostle denies the supposition of this type of assertion. God is not indifferent to what happens to our bodies : he raised Christ's from the dead. He attacks on two fronts : firstly, a person entering an illicit sexual union sets up a relationship of the flesh which profanes the present union with Christ in faith and baptism—which is a union of spirit; it shows that they have returned to the things of this world; secondly, the body itself is guaranteed to become 'spirit' because it is a temple of the Holy Spirit; a union of fornication destroys the future (eschatological) life the body is destined for.

These arguments make sense once we appreciate that the early Letters of Paul are dominated by the expectation that the new era of the Second Coming is just around the corner. Anything which cuts across the 'spiritual' character of the Christian's body must go, or that body (and its person) will have no share in Christian resurrection.

THIRD READING (JOHN 1:35-42)
They saw where he lived, and stayed with him

One of the disciples at this scene was probably the evangelist himself. On the surface, it is too simple a scene to have much theology behind it, but this would be most unusual in the Fourth Gospel.

There is not really any 'call' here—not until verse 43 (after this reading) do we hear this word. Nevertheless there is a call in the deepest sense of the word.

These men were John the Baptist's disciples. They have listened to his proclamation about the Messiah and obey the divinely inspired witness of John to commit themselves to the person John indicates. The Baptist is allowed by the evangelist to preach the sacrificial nature of the Messiah's mission. His witness to the 'Lamb of God' alludes to Jesus' hour of crucifixion. The Spirit already rests on Jesus and the disciples want to 'rest' where he does. Their calling is to follow and abide with Jesus. The nucleus of the Messiah's community is formed before any signs of his mission are given.

Thus the theme of obedience to God's call groups around itself the way we show this obedience. We listen to Jesus, we follow him and remain with him. Always there is utter conviction that he has what we want, and will show us what we really need—his are the words of eternal life.

Though the theme of discipleship and calling is not lacking on this Sunday, the repentance and conversion needed to receive God's blessing are more prominent.

The repentance of Nineveh at the preaching of Jonah is the classical conversion story. It fits in neatly with the highly schematized proclamation of Jesus in the first of the semi-continuous readings of Mark's Gospel. First Corinthians looks at marriage and virginity when Christ's coming is on the doorstep.

First Reading (Jonah 3:1-5. 10)

The people of Nineveh renounce their evil behaviour

Jonah is an extraordinary book. At a time when the people of Israel seemed intent on cutting themselves off from other peoples, this biblical 'novel' is published. It is a work of didactic or satirical fiction, based in all probability on Elijah's demand for the repentance of Israel. The remarkable point of the story is that Jonah succeeded in getting the Ninevites to repent.

Nineveh was a very large city; it became the capital of the Assyrian kings who destroyed Israel, and thus was a symbol of evil and enmity with God. Jonah gave forty days grace, reminding us of the days of the Flood when men did not repent. Jonah is upset at the success of his preaching! God should not be merciful to such an evil people. The reader will not forget that the chosen people did not repent when the prophets preached to them.

The Responsorial Psalm remembers the main point of the reading—the goodness and mercy of God towards sinners in teaching them his ways.

Second Reading (1 Corinthians 7:29-31)

The world as we know it is passing away

Though this passage continues the reading of First Corinthians, chapter 7 begins the second part of the Letter, which deals more with the questions sent to Paul by the Corinth community.

Paul's subject is marriage and virginity. Set into a chapter that tries to be practical are one or two of the dogmatic digressions very frequent in Paul's Letters. He is still quite convinced Christ will come very soon indeed. The time for people to repent and be saved is running out fast. Perhaps this is why Paul was in so much of a hurry to preach in a vast number of places.

Virginity is a good thing because it prepares more directly for the virginal state of the resurrection. Marriage is good, but it can distract from the urgent task on hand. Whatever position in life we have, keep to it; there is not time to worry about drastic changes in the direction of our earthly existence. Any kind of activity must be dropped if it undermines the preparation for the resurrection.

This Reading can be related to the other two through the stress on the urgency of conversion.

THIRD READING (MARK 1:14-20)

Repent, and believe the Good News

The first part of Mark's Gospel, once Jesus has been introduced (1:1-13), deals with the Messiahship of our Lord (1:14–8:33). It is also very much the period of the Galilean Ministry. Mark summarizes the content of Jesus' early preaching. He is more detailed than Matthew, whose equivalent verse is 'Repent, for the kingdom of heaven is close at hand' (Mt 3:17). For Mark, the kingdom being close at hand means that now is the time set by God for the Messiah to come. 'Repent' means more than 'go back to obeying the commandments of the Law'; it means, 'believe the Gospel'. Scholars talk about the eschatological nature of these verses: what God is doing in Jesus is his final word to man, the word which makes the whole creative purpose make sense; there is nothing else to wait for except the full-stop, when the world as we know it closes down.

Jesus calls his first disciples. Mark notes especially the privileged three, Peter, James and John, plus Andrew—like John's Gospel last week. Jesus seems to hold the majestic air of the divine presence, issuing the command for men to leave everything and follow him.

There is challenge in the tone of this Mass. It is a challenge to a repentance and conversion that means a total turning to the message God has sent us. Even the most hardened evil-doers can receive God's mercy through this message. Whenever the call of God to repentance is repeated it should always be tempered with the mercy he never ceases to show.

67

Jesus as a prophetic teacher is the theme of Sunday 4.

When Jesus taught, it was noticed that he did so with authority. The Old Testament foretold that God would send such a teacher in the shape of a prophet walking in the footsteps of Moses. In the continuous readings from First Corinthians, the virginal state is praised because it allows the Christian to give the Lord undivided attention.

FIRST READING (DEUTERONOMY 18:15-20)

I will raise up a prophet and I will put my words into his mouth

Divination and sorcery were facts of life in the ancient world. Israel was unique in refusing to adopt such procedures for controlling her God. Rather than her God bowing to her wishes, she had to be obedient to his. She learned what his decisions were through his own chosen mediators, the prophets. The criterion of the genuine prophet was his obedience to God's Word and Law, and the coming to pass of what he declared God would do.

Moses was the greatest mediator between Israel and her God, so that all prophets were to model themselves on him. Perhaps in the mind of the Deuteronomic author, it was Elijah that fulfilled the task of the prophet like Moses to be sent by God. But even Jewish tradition thought that this promise was still to be accomplished. That Jesus did fill the role is presumed by many of the Gospel texts.

To worship God, says the PSALM, means to follow faithfully the guidance he gives. We pray that we will not treat his words as the people of Israel treated his commands through his servant Moses.

SECOND READING (1 CORINTHIANS 7:32-35)

An unmarried woman can devote herself to the Lord's affairs; all she need worry about is being holy

This week's reading from First Corinthians carries on where last week's left off, but deals more explicitly with the question on hand—the value of marriage and virginity. Paul, who, remember, is convinced that the Lord's return is very near at hand, wants to help his converts see that married life can be a hindrance to paying the Lord due attention at this late hour. Virginity is precisely a characteristic of the last days because the future risen life is going to exclude the need for marriage (since procreation is excluded?). Married life necessarily roots one in the cares of this world. If this world is not going to last much longer, then the solution is obvious.

St Paul does not appear to specify virginity for a contemplative or missionary calling. He refers rather to the state of every Christian.

THIRD READING (MARK 1:21-28)
He taught them with authority

The first two verses are the most important in the Reading. They begin, summary fashion, the story of a typical day in Jesus' ministry. His activity points to his messianic character, but not inescapably. He may demonstrate his personal authority in word and deed, but prophets in the past were similarly inspired. His teaching did make an impression, but Mark shows later it is not the kind Jesus wanted. The people seemed to succumb to the danger of misinterpreting the type of Messiahship Jesus was going to show.

We have to remember that the reader of Mark's Gospel already knew who Jesus was. According to the evangelist, the unclean spirits cried out in agony at meeting a person so endowed with the Holy Spirit of God. His authority was not just that of any Rabbi, if the devils shrank from him.

It is interesting that Mark points out Jesus as *the* Teacher. Only Jesus teaches, yet Mark never tells us much of what he says. It is as if the healing and casting out of devils were illustrations of his *preaching*.

The Old Testament promised God would speak again in a new Moses. A new son of Israel would be the intermediary of a new covenant. When Jesus preaches things happen. His words make evil spirits flee. He is our teacher because he brought about what he preached. The Church follows in his footsteps by proclaiming the salvation she brings to men. Similarly, what makes the Christian tick, is what he professes in his faith.

69

FIFTH SUNDAY OF THE YEAR   *8 February 1970*

The memory of one of the early days in our Lord's preaching suggests a title for this Mass: A Laborious Day in Christ's Mission.

The Gospel is the story of twenty-four hours in Jesus' life—the closing phrase gives the impression of how tiring our Lord's messianic task would have been. The Reading from the Book of Job laments about the toil of a man's day. Even Paul tells about the efforts he has to make in his apostolic work.

FIRST READING (JOB 7:1-4. 6-7)

Restlessly I fret till twilight falls

Job continues his soliloquy of lament after the first conciliatory speech of Eliphaz. Job is a strange and beautiful book. It is the classic story of automatic religion versus personal, even passionate, encounter with God. With mounting acrimony, Job's friends say he must have sinned to deserve such wretchedness. Job says he hasn't—if God's friendship can mean such misery to man what is the point of making any effort.

The lot of the day-labourer, forced military service and simple slavery are the three classical wretched states of life in the ancient world. Job's life is like one of these.

Throughout the book, in spite of lines of great intimacy with God, there is no lessening of the conviction that earthly death is the final end of everything. It is strange to find this in a comparatively late book of the Old Testament. But it does explain why Job thinks God's help towards him might be too late.

THE RESPONSORIAL PSALM sings in answer to the gloom of Job. God understands all our labours and will finally lift us out of misery.

SECOND READING (1 CORINTHIANS 9:16-19. 22-23)

I should be punished if I did not preach the Gospel

First Corinthians has now moved on to another question. There were so many animals sacrificed in pagan temples that the temple priests had to sell the carcasses to butchers in the market. Could the Christian housewife buy it? Paul answers the way one might expect: 'Don't give scandal to the weaker brethren!'

70

Sewn into the delicacies of this problem are many other topics. Paul is not afraid to point to himself as worthy of imitation—this isn't the last time he does it in his Letters.

To make himself a more acceptable messenger of salvation, he was prepared to renounce his apostolic privileges. He does not even want to think of his rights, but is dominated by his duty to preach, come what may. Becoming all things to all men is like making oneself a slave. The slave-servant motif would hardly be without allusion to the Servant Status of his Master. In spite of failures, he must carry on to gain his share in the Gospel he preaches. These are some of the most incisive of all Paul's words on his apostolic office.

THIRD READING (MARK 1:29-39)

He cured many who were suffering from diseases of one kind and another

In this reading we sense the pressure on our Lord. It is remarkable how Mark can tell us so much in so few words. He gives the impression that Jesus is invading a hostile world—unclean spirits and illnesses seem to exclude the presence of God. When Jesus enters this atmosphere there is so much to do. Mark knows this. That is why he gives the (first) twenty-four hour programme of Jesus in action, whose messianic power seems to have no limits. But this power has its dangers, false messianic hopes and nationalistic demonstrations. Mark gives an indication of the likelihood of these dangers. When Jesus goes to pray, he expresses his submission to his Father's will. He is refusing to capitalize on his day's work at Capernaum. Jesus spots the wrong attitude present even in his disciples. This gives the evangelist the cue he needs to show that Jesus went preaching elsewhere, and reveal the type of effect he had everywhere as 'he went all through Galilee, preaching in their synagogues and casting out devils' (1:39, the summary verse).

The Mass shows several attitudes towards work: drudgery, compulsion, enthusiasm for God's service. Paul imitates Jesus in being consumed with the desire to spread God's message. The work of a Christian is not to thrust Christianity down people's throats, but to become all things to all men to win them for God, who calls men in a way which respects personal freedom.

71

The Paschal Cycle

Ash Wednesday (11 February 1970) — Pentecost (17 May 1970)

THE SEASON OF LENT

Directive from the Council

When the Constitution on the Sacred Liturgy talks about the liturgical year (chapter five), it singles out Lent for a special paragraph. This is best quoted in full to show the tone of the Council's mind:

'The Lenten season has a two-fold character:
1) it recalls baptism and prepares for it;
2) it stresses a penitential spirit.

By these means especially, Lent readies the faithful to celebrate the paschal mystery after a period of closer attention to the Word of God, and more ardent prayer. In the liturgy itself and in liturgy-centred instructions, these baptismal and penitential themes should be more pronounced. Hence:

(a)   Wider use is to be made of the baptismal features proper to the Lenten liturgy; some elements which belonged to a now-lapsed tradition may be opportunely restored.

(b)   The same approach holds for the penitential element. As regards instruction, it is important to impress on the minds of the faithful not only the social consequences of sin but also the fact that the real essence of the virtue of penance is hatred for sin as an offence against God; the role of the Church in penitential practices is not to be passed over, and the people must be exhorted to pray for sinners (no. 109).'

In the Lectionary

It is especially in the readings that the Council mandate is applied to the Mass.

From early times, great emphasis was laid, in the preparation for baptism, on the account of the history of salvation. It is true that Christ's death and resurrection brought a new and eternal covenant, but God's other covenants deliniate the way God acts for men. Consequently, the Church remembers the covenants of the Old Testament in her preparation for Easter to remind the faithful of the stages of God's plan for our redemption, as well as to instruct those to be baptized. The Old Testament Readings on the Sundays of Lent recall the covenants with Noah, Abraham, Moses and Israel, the restoration from exile (in Year Two) and the promise of the new covenant.

There should be great hesitation in omitting these Old Testament passages. Second Readings are chosen because they correspond as much as possible with the Old Testament and Gospel texts.

For the first two Sundays, the Gospel Readings remain as in the previous Missal, the Temptation and the Transfiguration. For the other three Sundays, before Palm Sunday, the great chapters of John's Gospel that are traditionally associated with faith and baptism have been restored: the dialogue with the Samaritan woman, the cure of the man born blind, the raising of Lazarus. These three chapters are the special readings of Year One, but they, like the other two readings of Year One, may be used in all three years of the cycle.

In Year Two, the proper readings are texts from John as beautiful and as fitting as the three of Year One, but perhaps not so identified with Lenten Sundays in liturgical tradition. They are the cleansing of the Temple, the dialogue with Nicodemus and the 'grain of wheat' discourse as Jesus approaches his hour.

In the Calendar

1. Lent lasts from Ash Wednesday until the start of the Evening Mass on Holy Thursday. Ash Wednesday, however, is not included in the Sunday Lectionary.
2. Throughout Lent, as in the previous Missal, Alleluia is not used with the versicle of the Gospel Acclamation. The cantor chooses his own acclamation to precede the versicle, from several given in the Lectionary, e.g. 'Praise and glory to you, Lord Jesus'.
3. Passiontide has been suppressed. Lenten Sundays number one to five. The sixth begins Holy Week; its Latin title is: *Dominica in Palmis de Passione Domini.*

Both the Lenten themes of baptism and penance are here.

The Gospel reminds us that the Passion of our Lord is a struggle against the powers of evil. The saving of Noah from the waters of the flood begins a new human era and brings a fresh promise from God. First Peter shows the relationship of Noah, Christian baptism and Christ's resurrection.

FIRST READING (GENESIS 9:8-15)

God's covenant with Noah, after he had saved him from the waters of the flood

This Reading comes from one of the most recent strands of the Pentateuchal traditions that make up the first five books of the Bible. Priest writers incorporated their centuries-old traditions into the story of the Flood. Their theological viewpoint centred around eras and covenants. The covenant implicit in the creation story was broken by sin. So the covenant with Noah, likewise made with all men, recognizes the reign of sin as a fact. Yet God pledges that he will no longer use natural phenomena to punish mankind. The ancient appeasing rainbow of the gods is declared by the priestly author to be the sign of the only God's universal covenant.

THE RESPONSORIAL PSALM is an individual petition asking God to teach the Psalmist his ways, even though he is a sinner. The faithfulness and love of the Response is *the* Old Testament characteristic of God, faithful to his covenant with Moses.

SECOND READING (1 PETER 3:18-22)

That water is a type of the baptism which saves you now

The whole flood episode has led Christian writers to reflect on the story as the prefiguring of Baptism. It is to be expected that First Peter, admitted to be a baptismal sermon-letter, should refer back to 'Noah . . . saved through water'.

Peter wants to instil perseverance in the face of persecution. To do this he puts before his hearers the triumphant resurrection of Christ as it effects themselves and all creation. Christians are associated with the resurrection by *passing through* water. (The parallel is obviously stretched, as Noah was hardly saved except by being in the Ark.) Baptism is not first and foremost the external water, but the recognition of the conscience or 'confession of faith' of the believer.

So difficult to interpret is the 'preaching to the spirits in prison'. A view most in agreement with the context would seem to be : as Christ passed up through the heavens to the highest throne of God, he made his resurrection known to all imprisoned spirits, not so much to save them as to declare his universal dominion.

THIRD READING (MARK 1:12-15)

Jesus was tempted by Satan, and the angels looked after him

The few verses of the Reading are central to the understanding of Mark's Gospel. Jesus has been given his mission by the Father and the Spirit. Immediately Mark expresses what this mission is all about : the hidden war with Satan goes on at the same time as the outward proclamation of his message.

In the temptation scene it is incorrect to interpret Mark with Matthew's and Luke's longer accounts in mind. The Spirit has impelled Jesus into the lair of Satan, the wilderness. There he has to engage in the battle that is to continue in the lives of Christians. But already the victory is assured. The presence of the Spirit, the ministry of angels, his peace with the wild beasts point to a reversal of sin's reign in the world.

Jesus' preaching during his public ministry in Galilee is summarized in verse 15. It has the flavour of the 'final days', as does the Temptation scene. God's final reign is on the doorstep; past ages are coming to the final definitive stage. All men can do is to change their whole personality and be converted from sinful ways. Conversion is faith. Believe, while there is still time! This summary verse will be explained in the Gospel. Jesus is the promised Messiah. In him God's plan is achieved. Men must believe in him to be converted.

Another strand of the Mass, which originates from the baptismal and penitential streams, concerns the cosmic significance of man's relationship with God. If man sins, the world is affected, as it was in the time of the Flood. When Christ comes, evil powers are disbanded and the world released from their grip. But until the final universal upheaval that marks God's seal on his plan, the confession of faith that leads to baptism is what makes the new covenant come into being. Only when men are really ready for God, will the rest of creation follow.

SECOND SUNDAY OF LENT   *22 February 1970*

The relationship of Father and Son is very much the concern of the Mass texts today.

The Gospel is the story of the transfiguration, a prefiguring of the resurrection. The sacrifice of Isaac by his father Abraham is the poignant symbol of what Paul tells us in the Second Reading. God stopped the final blow of Abraham on Isaac, but did not spare his own Son when our salvation needed his sacrifice.

FIRST READING (GENESIS 22:1-2. 9-13. 15-18)
The sacrifice of our father Abraham, our Father in faith

The sacrifice of Isaac, told in the very much abridged version of the First Reading, forms the climax of Abraham's life and faith. It is a simple but mysterious story told by the prophetic tradition of the northern Israelite kingdom (Elohist Tradition). Time and place are not important.

Once the religious message is appreciated various shades of meaning appear. The story supports the continual condemnation in the Old Testament of human and child sacrifice. Isaac was the child of God's promise and so belonged to him. All first-born male children had, in later practice, to be 'bought back' from God. Lastly, the story confirms the value of complete trust and confidence in God.

For the Christian reader the words to Abraham, 'Take your son, your only child Isaac, whom you love', can only refer to the New Testament descriptions of Jesus as God's only-begotten Son. Isaac was redeemed by a ram, but God handed his Son over as a redemption for all men.

THE RESPONSORIAL PSALM also takes up the theme of sacrifice, as the Psalmist offers a sacrifice of thanksgiving to God, who has rescued him from terrible danger.

SECOND READING (ROMANS 8:31-34)
God did not spare his own Son

Very often in the Epistle to the Romans, Abraham is used as an example. As Abraham did not think to spare Isaac, 'God did not spare his own Son, but gave him up to benefit us all'.

Romans, chapter eight, is one of the most beautiful as well as most theological chapters of the New Testament. Paul talks about the Christian as the child of God and the home of the Holy Spirit.

With a hymn of hope and love, Paul sums up his chapter and indeed the whole Epistle so far. The Reading today contains only the first verse of this two-verse hymn.

The condemnation of God, on Jew and Pagan alike, has been lifted from those who believe in the Gospel. No human persecutions or judgments can alter his favour on the man of faith. How could it be otherwise if it is his only Son who died for us and rose to intercede for us? It puts the Christian into an entirely new situation—he possesses the Spirit of the Father and Christ. And Christ continues to intercede for him at his Father's right hand.

THIRD READING (MARK 9:1-9)
This is my Son, the Beloved

Peter's confession that Jesus was God's Messiah, the first prediction of the passion and resurrection and the transfiguration seem in Mark's Gospel to form one single event. It would mean that the transfiguration is the divine guarantee that Jesus is the Messiah, and the ratification of Jesus' declared purpose to suffer and die. God demands that men *listen* to his beloved Son.

Mark's account is two-directional. There is a presence of God on the same pattern as those of the Old Testament; see especially Exodus 24 : the high mountain, Moses and Elijah, the voice, the overshadowing cloud, even the six days. On the other hand, Mark is clearly looking forward to the future final Day; unearthly brightness and whiteness (represented in the later tradition of the white garments worn after baptism), the tents, representing God's 'tenting' among men, with his saints.

Most of all, the glory of Jesus anticipates his resurrection and exaltation, an anticipation also intended in the liturgy. The disciples are brought down to earth again. There is much to be endured before the glory of Jesus and the final glory of God's presence among men can be brought about.

How are the baptismal and penitential themes made clear? Baptism makes the man of faith a child of God. It means he must listen to God's only-begotten, accepting that his submission to the Father's will may demand a similar supreme sacrifice. But he is convinced that a sacrifice offered in faith will bring to himself and to others the blessings that belong to the Beloved. God has done so much for us; he also demands that we become more acceptable to himself. Therefore, we take notice of his Son.

The theme of the Mass centres around the old dispensation of God and its replacement by the revelation and sacrifice of Christ.

The Gospel shows Jesus as the new Temple, replacing the old one which had failed in its task. (To the Samaritan Woman, Jesus appeals to a worship in spirit and truth.) The way God brought about his new covenant was through the crucified Christ —a plan only his wisdom could devise. The commandments of the old Law have been superceded by the greatest blessing of God, his full self-revelation through his Son.

Note that on this Sunday and for the Fourth and Fifth Sundays of Lent the readings from Year One can replace the proper Readings of Year Two. Here, we will comment only on the Gospels of Year One because of their Lenten importance.

FIRST READING (EXODUS 20:1-17)
The Law was given through Moses

Important though the promises to Abraham were, the cardinal dogma of Old Testament religion was: 'God led his people out of Egypt.' He chose them as his own, he rescued them and entered into covenant with them. Always this covenant must be seen as a gratuitous action of God on behalf of his 'vassal' people. In a treaty of friendship, he tells them who he is, what he has done for them and the kind of loyalty he requires.

The Ten Commandments, God's Ten Words, are the requirements he lays down. They are face to face with a God who is not arbitrary or callous, not nationalistic or distant from their affairs. He is just, moral, all-powerful, close to his chosen people.

Are these commandments just natural law? Rather, they reflect a nomadic family morality. Both Jew and Christian developed them to fit the situations of later ages.

THE RESPONSORIAL PSALM sings the praises of God's glory as seen in his Law, with the Response of Peter's faith in the 'new words' of life spoken by Christ. The Psalmist pledges his loyalty and begs protection against unwittingly offending God.

SECOND READING (1 CORINTHIANS 1:22-25)
Here we are preaching a crucified Christ, an obstacle to men, but to those who are called, the wisdom of God

Paul is not condemning the Jews for asking for signs, nor the

78

Pagans (Greeks) for seeking explanations of the world and for life. Our Lord worked signs and explained what life is all about. Rather, Paul is pillorying an attitude that is evident also among the Corinthians. It is their unwillingness to recognize the way God wants things done; a demand that God should fit the requirements and explanations they feel should be right. For a Jew, the Law is wisdom; for a Greek wisdom is philosophy. But God's wisdom is not like those things any more. It is the cross of Christ through which divine power flows into the world as never before. Through the cross, God has given the greatest sign and revealed the highest purpose in life. Notice that the cross in Paul means the total salvation event : from the passion to the gift of the Holy Spirit.

THIRD READING (JOHN 2:13-25)
Destroy this sanctuary, and in three days I will raise it up

In John signs are only important if they lead to faith in who and what Jesus is. The Cleansing of the Temple is the sign that clarifies the Hour of Jesus just mentioned in the Cana sign; it is the death and resurrection of Christ. Even the disciples grasp this only after the Easter events. Much more than in the other Gospels, John has to be interpreted backwards; the meaning of each event is seen in the light of Christ's glorification. The great Jewish Passover worship, and even the temple itself, is to be replaced by a new spiritual and universal worship which Jesus himself first offers at his Hour. His own body is destroyed and rebuilt in the resurrection. Those who believe henceforward worship God through the Glorified Jesus.

[In the dialogue with the Samaritan woman—*ad libitum* from Year One—similar themes appear. In his Hour, Jesus becomes the fountain of living water, the one in whom spiritual worship is offered to God, the prophet like Moses' and Israel's awaited Messiah.]

In spite of the great blessing of God's Ten Words in the Old Testament, these commandments represent only a preparation. Their stipulations can only be met in the faith and grace of *the* Blessing of God, his crucified and risen Son. The baptismal theme is thus brought out in the incorporation of men into Christ's Body, when his glorified life is shared out to those who believe. The penitential theme appears in the giving up of the old life patterns to enter into even closer identity with the source of God's blessing.

79

God so loved us, though we were sinners, that he handed over Jesus to death. The theme of this Mass speaks of this love of God for sinful men.

In the Gospel, Jesus is to be lifted up, because God has loved the world so much that he wanted to save it by what is most precious to him. Though the Exile in Babylon was for the people of Israel a punishment for centuries of covenant breaking, God brought them to a newer and deeper life after it had ended. Similarly, God's mercy reached to us sinners to give a fresh and eternal life through the resurrection of his Son.

FIRST READING (2 CHRONICLES 36:14-16. 19-23)
The wrath and mercy of God are revealed in the exile and in the release of his people

Coolly but dramatically the Chronicler sums up the exile and restoration of Israel (587–538 BC). The whole nation had been so scornfully disobedient to the warnings God gave through his prophets. The three things most dear to the Chronicler came under the hand of God. The *Temple* is destroyed and worship there ceases. The *Land* is uninhabited and desolate. God punishes the profanation of his *Sabbath* by a sabbath of decades in exile.

But Yahweh inspired the Great King Cyrus to restore the Temple. God will now be with his people as they go up to the Holy City and into the Temple itself. God will be present among them again.

THE RESPONSORIAL PSALM sings of the memory of Jerusalem among the exiles, and curses those who forget her.

SECOND READING (EPHESIANS 2:4-10)
You who were dead through your sins, have been saved through grace

Rather than the nationalistic attitude of Chronicles, Ephesians proclaims the salvation of all men. The separating wall between Jews and Pagans has been taken down by Christ. *Already* things have happened because of the redemption Christ brought: Jew and pagan have already been given the gifts of resurrection and redemption; already we are saved by the free gift of God's love.

80

This passage from Ephesians is noted for its past tenses and 'have been's'. But these past gifts continue; they come in abundance from the hand of God as utterly freely as when we were first saved from our sins. To believe in Christ is to share in his life and work, to belong among the redeemed.

THIRD READING (JOHN 3:14-21)
God sent his Son, so that through him the world might be saved

The dialogue with Nicodemus is saturated with the theme of faith in Jesus. The Lord reveals himself to a man who believes in the signs he works, but this is not sufficient. A new birth is needed, a birth in water and the Holy Spirit that comes through faith.

To realize that John sees all the events of Jesus' life in the light of his final Hour of Glorification will explain the finality of tone in this passage. When Moses lifted up the brazen serpent in the desert, the people who had been bitten by the fiery serpents sent by God to punish them, could *look at* the bronze serpent and live. Similarly those who gaze at Jesus enthroned on the cross will be saved and gain eternal life because they look in faith.

John rarely uses the term 'world' in a neutral sense. But here it is the object of God's love in so far as it accepts his Son in faith. Otherwise it is condemned and becomes the sum-total of unbelief and the symbol of forces opposed to God. The only replies to Jesus' revelation and God's love are faith or unbelief. The fact that it is God who has acted means indifference is impossible.

[The cure of the blind man—*ad libitum* from Year One—acts out the same kind of theme in much clearer terms. Jesus is the light of the world, yet is met with such blindness—a perverse sort of blindness we might say. But for John this is just the mystery of unbelief. To the man who came to Jesus and defended him before unbelievers, Jesus gives internal as well as external light. He becomes one of Jesus' Own.]

The baptismal theme is vivid in the dialogue with Nicodemus. God's love for men who believe in his Son is boundless. They receive the Spirit in the Waters of Baptism, so that everything the baptized do bears the stamp of God's grace. But the experience of Israel shows that God's love has to purify those who have slipped from the integrity of baptismal faith, by bringing them back into the light of Christ. Hence the need for a penitential strand to this season of baptismal preparation.

81

In the liturgy of this Mass, the Hour of Jesus is fast approaching.

The humble submission of Jesus to his Father's will is paramount in the Gospel of the grain of wheat. The mood is more controlled than in the other readings. Jeremiah, so often the prophet of God's anger, preaches a new covenant with a new and unparalleled intimacy with God. The author of the Epistle to the Hebrews is in the heart of his theology: our great high priest came to obey through his sufferings.

FIRST READING (JEREMIAH 31:31-34)
I will make a new covenant and never call their sin to mind

Long has it been recognized that these verses are the 'spiritual testimony' of Jeremiah. They put the emphasis on the divine judgment, so much the soul of his mission, into a wider context of God's greater plan for the future. The Old Testament talks elsewhere of an eternal covenant, with a new heart and a new spirit in God's people. But nowhere else is there talk of a *new* covenant.

What is new about a covenant, when God, the people and obedience to his Law remain the same? Newness comes when the relationship between man and God becomes more interior and personal. Each man is taught by God in his innermost being; he has his sins forgiven and is required to love and obey from the depths of his heart. Only then will this be a new covenant, with a new heart and a new spirit.

Anxiousness for the forgiveness of sins characterizes this penitential Psalm *par excellence* used for the RESPONSORIAL PSALM. The Psalmist realizes that only religion of the heart pleases God.

SECOND READING (HEBREWS 5:7-9)
He learnt to obey and became the source of eternal salvation

Many times in Hebrews the author stresses the exaltation of Christ only to return to his humiliation. This time he does it in reference to the high priesthood of Christ. First comes the definition of what high priesthood means. A man is chosen from among men by God; it has to be a man so that he may know what the sufferings of his fellow men really are.

Rather than stressing the divinity of Christ, Hebrews is more concerned with Christ lifted up to God's throne through the anguish and suffering of a human life. In his suffering he prayed to be raised up by God even from death.

In these verses, the author sums up what he is going to discuss in the central part of his work (5:11–10:18). Jesus learned submission to God's will; he was an acceptable sacrifice, being 'made perfect'. Thus accepted by his Father, he became the source of eternal life to all who submit to him in faith.

THIRD READING (JOHN 12:20-33)
If a grain of wheat falls on the ground and dies, it yields a rich harvest

Throughout his Gospel so far, John has stressed that the Hour of Jesus has not yet come. Now comes the change—the Hour is at hand.

Greeks come to Jesus. The Pharisees interpret this for us—'the whole world is running after him'. But Jesus is concerned with his own death. Far from being the empty corruption of the body, it is for him the glorification of his Father, the lifting up of himself on the cross. The love of his Father draws all men towards his cross. All men can gaze at him on this throne of glory and be saved.

[The moving story of Lazarus—*ad libitum* from Year One— tells of a death that is for the glory of God. It illustrates the resurrection and the life given by Jesus. As a sign of the glory that will be given to God by the death of Jesus, it is also the sign of the conquering faith of the man who believes. As such it is a sign of the risen life of baptism.]

The baptismal themes come fast and furious as the Paschal mysteries approach. The passage from Hebrews epitomizes the ambivalence of the liturgy: the suffering of Christ versus the magnitude of our salvation. The Gospel admits that the perfect calm of Jesus is broken by thoughts of the Hour, even when the outcome is clear. Baptism brings us into intimacy with God; it opens up the treasures of eternal salvation, but not without the pains and dilemmas of the road to faith. The message of Christ demands we come close to him. This means greater faith and a greater share in the path he took to gain it for us.

PASSION SUNDAY (*Palm Sunday*)   *22 March 1970*

PROCESSIONAL READING (*Either* MARK 11:1-10 *or* JOHN 12:12-16)
Blessings on him who comes in the name of the Lord

Mark: The triumphal entry into the Holy City begins the account of Jesus' Jerusalem ministry, during which Mark seems intent on accumulating a number of Jesus' words and deeds that reveal the blindness of the Jewish leaders.

Again there is much irony in the story of Jesus' entry. The shout of the people rings better as, 'Blessed in the name of the Lord be he that comes . . .' It could point to any pilgrim coming up for the festival. The Christian recognizes Jesus as God's envoy, glorified now, but then doomed by the people's lack of faith. Since the crowds miss the allusion to the messianic humility of Jesus, riding an ass, they fail to understand that he must suffer.

John: There are no illusions in John's account about the messianic kingship of Jesus in this procession. The enthusiasm of the crowds had been stirred up by the raising of Lazarus. The authorities were upset enough over this Lazarus incident, but now there is utter dismay, when 'the whole world is running after him'.

However, there is little secular about this scene in John. Jesus is the messianic king of peace and humility. Mark's allusion becomes in John the explicit quotation of Zechariah's prophecy (9:9) about the humble king who will be pierced. Once again John confesses that the disciples did not see the point until after Jesus' glorification. We too see it in the light of the paschal event.

AT MASS

Holy Week themes flood this Mass. The third of Isaiah's Servant Songs introduces the theme of suffering. The great christological hymn of the Letter to the Philippians is read, telling of the humiliation of Christ. The traditional reading of a Passion Narrative is continued; being Year Two, it is from Mark's Gospel. There is the strongest recommendation to read all three texts.

The theme of the Mass is the sufferings of our Lord.

FIRST READING (ISAIAH 50:4-7)

I did not cover my face against insult—I know I shall not be shamed

The Third Servant Song of Second Isaiah introduces the idea

84

that the Servant is to suffer. He experiences the lot of the prophets. God's Word encompasses him whether he is well or weary, sleeping or awake. His message from God is met with rejection, and treated with insult. But God is at his side; he can stand firm.

THE RESPONSORIAL PSALM has the traditional Psalm for Holy Week. Very much in the spirit of Isaian Servant Songs, it tells of the Psalmist's sufferings and praises God for his deliverance.

SECOND READING (PHILIPPIANS 2:6-11)
He humbled himself, but God raised him high

This beautiful hymn is a signature tune of Holy Week. It summarizes not just the divine mysteries of this week, but also the whole question 'Who is Christ?'. Paul inserted this hymn to call to mind the humble attitude needed for any true unity among Christians. It must be based on Christ's humble, free submission.

What constituted Christ's humiliation? Is it the incarnation itself, or the assuming of the particular humanity he did in fact accept? In the present liturgical context, it is the identity with human suffering which was the true humiliation. This supreme obedience was the cause of his exaltation as Lord of all creation.

THIRD READING (MARK 14:1-15:47)
The Passion of our Lord Jesus Christ

Mark's Gospel has been described as a Passion narrative with a long introduction. Note its simplicity and theological drama.

Jesus is alone as Suffering Servant. He gives himself up for all men. He claims unequivocally the highest prerogatives, when he is solemnly questioned about himself by the High Priest. Even Peter and the others desert him. There is irony in every verse— 'He saved others! He cannot save himself!' Judgment comes upon the old covenant for its final disbelief, and the gentiles in the mouth of the centurion now come to accept its saviour. Mark's narrative conveys the mystery of belief and unbelief, of humility and the highest of achievements.

Though this Mass is devoted to the sufferings of our Lord, the theme of successful endurance also appears. His was not the ultimate misery of suffering for a lost cause. His case was won before he undertook the Passion. It is the same for the Christian, though he knows that the road to eternal life will not avoid the road to Calvary. Thus suffering shows the theme of penance, and its successful outcome the final scope of Christian baptism.

THE CHRISM MASS OF HOLY THURSDAY

26 March 1970

On the morning of Holy Thursday, the Bishop celebrates with his priests the Mass of the Holy Oils. This is the closing Mass of the Lenten Season.

This Chrism Mass has for its theme Jesus, the anointed one of God.

In the passage from Luke's Gospel used in the Third Reading, the text of the First Reading, from Isaiah, is used by our Lord for a homily which opens his public life—he has come anointed with God's Holy Spirit. The Apocalypse pictures the glorified Jesus making his people like himself, kings and priests in God's service.

FIRST READING (ISAIAH 61:1-3. 6. 8-9)

The Lord has anointed me and has sent me to bring good news to the poor, and to give them the oil of gladness

The Isaian prophet is anointed by the spirit of God to bring the message of salvation to the exiles who have returned home. Their sufferings and distress will blossom out into the joy of being set free. Their freedom will now give them the title of priests and ministers of God. His everlasting covenant with them becomes the visible sign of his blessing on them, for the whole world to see.

THE RESPONSORIAL PSALM sings of the prerogatives of the Davidic King-Messiah. He will be the anointed and receive the gift of adoption as the son of God.

SECOND READING (APOCALYPSE 1:5-8)

He made us a line of kings, priests to serve his God and Father

The kingly and priestly qualities of Christ and his people are especially brought out in this Greeting to the Churches of Asia. The Churches are saluted by their Lord who loves them so much that he shed his blood in sacrifice for them. He is king, priest and Son. What he is, his people will become.

Though men persecuted him, he will show he is king. There will be no more doubt when he returns as Lord and Judge of the universe.

Jesus is portrayed in terms which describe God in the Old Testament. He has history in his hands. There is no need for his own to worry any longer, for he will not fail them.

The sacrificial blood of Christ is the life-spring of all the signs and sacraments used in the Church for men's salvation.

THIRD READING (LUKE 4:16-21)

The Spirit of the Lord has been given to me, for he has anointed me

The synagogue service at the time of Christ was probably structured thus:
1. Two Prayers—The *Shemoneh Esreh* (18 Benedictions)
2. Two Readings: (i) from the Law, and (ii) from the Prophets
3. The homily
4. The Priestly Blessing (Numbers 6:22-27).

Jesus as a mature Jew was asked to give the homily. So he chose his prophetic text from Isaiah. As the spirit was given to the prophets, this same spirit continues in himself. Luke has just told his readers that the Spirit took Jesus over at the Baptism, and now directs his whole mission. His life-work is consecrated by God for all those in need, physically and spiritually. His message for them is the Good News of Salvation.

In the Chrism Mass, the Church commemorates the Spirit being given to the Church in her sacraments. The oil which symbolically anointed Jesus as King, Priest and Prophet becomes after his glorification the sign of consecration, purification and joy. This Mass anticipates the celebrations of the next three days, and indeed the whole of Paschaltide. It becomes the special task of the bishop to commemorate what he represents—the Ruling, Priestly and Teaching office of Christ.

THE EASTER TRIDUUM

The centre of the Church's Year is the Easter Triduum. It begins with the Evening Mass of Holy Thursday, reaches its climax in the Mass of the Paschal Vigil, and closes with the Vespers of Easter Sunday.

The liturgical year celebrates the whole mystery of Christ, but its high point is the paschal mysteries, when the time came for Jesus to return to his Father and accomplish our salvation. As Sunday is the Lord's Day of the Week, so the Sacred Triduum is the Lord's Time of the Year.

The Paschal Vigil culminates the liturgy of the three days as the most Sacred Night of our Lord's Resurrection—the central act of redemption, from which the life and sacraments of the Church originate. The liturgy consequently pours out all her riches for the paschal night—the most sacred readings of scripture, the sacraments of baptism, (confirmation) and the holy eucharist, and the total renewal of the Christian commitment to the Risen Lord.

Themes in the Lectionary

The Commemoration of the Last Supper uses the traditional passages for the Second and Third Readings. It is the sacrificial aspect that envelops within itself the sacramental and eucharistic themes. In the Gospel, Jesus teaches the example of submissive obedience to the Father's will. This is the essence of his sacrifice, for in this he shows his boundless love for his own that leads to him giving a sacramental memorial of his sacrifice. Paul's classic text from First Corinthians interprets the meaning of the Last Supper for all Christ's Body. The Old Testament seals the sacrificial theme by referring to the meal which preceded the greatest of God's Old Testament deeds, the Exodus from Egypt —the Exodus theme returns in the Paschal Vigil.

The *Good Friday Liturgy* concentrates on the humiliation and suffering of Christ. The last of Isaiah's Servant Songs tells of the intense sufferings of the Servant, that all men might be saved. For the Christian this Song must number among the greatest pages of the Old Testament. The theologian-author of the Epistle to the Hebrews is not slow to point out the real sufferings of Christ in obedience to his Father's command. These two passages give something of a tone of anguish to the sublime Jesus of John's Passion, where humble submission is paramount. An air of inevitability surrounds John's proceedings; if men refuse to believe in him this is what happens.

'He is risen', our redemption is assured! The *Paschal Vigil* is a cry of victory. The Lectionary gives nine readings for the Paschal Vigil; seven from the Old Testament, of which at least three are to be read (or in cases of exceptional pastoral urgency, only two); then the Epistle and Gospel. The Old Testament readings cover the whole sweep of Salvation history: 1. The creation, 2. The sacrifice of Abraham, 3. The exodus (this reading is obligatory), 4–5. The redemption from exile and the eternal covenant, 6. The way of God in his Law, 7. The cleansing from sin and the new heart. It would be best to take at least one of the readings from the Prophets (4–7); Readings 1, 3 and 7 could be suggested if only three are to be used. The baptismal chapter of Romans interprets the meaning of the night: eternal death is no longer part of us, because Christ is risen from the dead and raises us with him into a new life. The Gospel is light and joyful; it is the story of the Empty Tomb. The door of the new world is opened—'He is Risen'.

The *Mass of Easter Day* completes the Sacred Triduum and already introduces the joy of Paschaltide. Christ's victory is more than enough to make us forget the efforts needed to become more like him. The readings from Acts are commenced, replacing the Old Testament readings until Pentecost. Peter's final sermon gives us the typical early proclamation of the resurrection. The Epistle asks us to live a life worthy of the risen, celestial Christ. The Gospel narrates John's version of the empty tomb story and the disciples finally see the point of everything—they come to believe.

THE SEASON OF PASCHALTIDE

In the early Church, Paschaltide was thought of as the Great Sunday of the liturgical year, a continuation of the Paschal Triduum, making one great festival of joy in the Risen Christ. (This was probably inspired by the fact that seven weeks out of fifty-two make one in seven, like the Sunday in the rest of the week.)

The Sundays after Easter are now to be called Sundays of Easter, to lay more stress on the continuity of Easter. There are thus seven Sundays of Easter, Easter Day being itself included.

The Feast of the Ascension is held forty days after Easter, following the tradition taken from Acts 1:3; but provision is made for the Feast to be transferred to the final Sunday before Pentecost in places where it is not a Holy Day of Obligation.

Themes of Paschaltide

Rejoicing in the company of the risen Lord is the major theme of this season. But others stem from it: communion of life with God, unity among Christians, the coming of the Holy Spirit and the mission of the disciples to the world.

In the Lectionary

The ancient liturgical practice of reading the Acts of the Apostles during Paschaltide is now restored. It replaces Old Testament passages in the First Reading. In each year of the cycle, there is a representative selection of passages from Acts, whether examples of the early Church's preaching, or passages about her early life and progress.

In Year Two, there are readings from Peter's Sermons (on four Sundays), one progress report and an account of the effect of Paul's conversion. The sections of Acts 1–2 which refer to the Ascension, Pentecost and the time between are used on the respective feasts and the intervening Sunday.

The First Epistle of John is read semi-continuously on all the Sundays of Easter from two to seven of Year Two. The Lectionary considers this Letter one of *the* paschal writings, unfolding as it does the new life in faith and love which the Christian should live as a child of God.

Texts from Colossians (Easter Sunday) and Ephesians (Ascension Day) describe the glories of the Risen and Exalted Christ, while passages from Romans and First Corinthians are employed to teach the place of the Spirit in Christian life, on the Vigil of Pentecost and Pentecost Day itself.

John's Gospel predominates in Paschaltide. Two out of the three passages used to recall the appearances of our Lord, on Easter Day and the two successive Sundays, are taken from John 20.

Good Shepherd Sunday now becomes the Fourth Sunday of Easter, not the Second Sunday after Easter as in the previous Missal. The Good Shepherd discourse is read in separate sections over the three years of the cycle, as are the Farewell discourses of Jesus and the Priestly Prayer, from Sunday Five to Sunday Seven of Easter. The intimacy of Jesus with his own in these chapters of John make them eminently suitable for this season.

John's is also the Gospel of Pentecost Day, when the formal giving of the Spirit from John chapter 20 is heard, and on the Vigil of the feast, when we are reminded that Jesus will pour out the Spirit on those who come to him.

On the Feast of the Ascension, in each year of the cycle the missionary mandate of Christ to his apostles is given in the version of the predominent Gospel—in 1970 it is Mark's account.

Like Christmas and Easter, Pentecost has a Vigil Mass; a selection of four Old Testament texts are set for this evening Mass, recalling principal Pentecost themes : the dispersion and reunification of mankind, the covenant at Sinai, the Spirit reviving the people and being poured out on all God's children.

HOLY THURSDAY: MASS OF THE LORD'S SUPPER

The theme of the Last Supper Commemoration is the sacrifice of Christ for love of us. The eucharist is left us as a memorial, the sacramental sacrifice of Christ in his Church.

In the Gospel Jesus instructs his own by showing them the example of his submissiveness to his Father's will. He becomes the new Paschal Lamb. By sharing in this Lamb, the new people of God share in the redemption it brings. Paul witnesses to the early liturgy of the eucharist as the memorial of Christ's death.

FIRST READING (EXODUS 12:1-8. 11-14)
Instructions concerning the Passover meal

The importance of the Passover or Pasch for Israel comes from its relation to the greatest act of God's mercy, the leading of his people out of Egypt. The sacrifice of the Lamb without blemish warded off the angel of destruction that descended on Egypt to bring about the terrible Tenth Plague. All the Egyptian first-born were to be slain, but not those of the Israelites who ate the lamb and sprinkled its blood on the doorposts of their homes.

The Pasch re-enacts that exodus night in the worship of a sacrificial meal. Many see the Pasch as the historicizing of two ancient festivals, the sacrificing of the first fruits of the flocks and the offering of the first grains of barley.

Whatever its origin, it becomes a ritual that is fulfilled in the sacrament of the eucharist when the sacrificial blood of Christ flows, under the symbols of bread and wine.

THE RESPONSORIAL PSALM offers thanksgiving to God in the offering of a sacrifice.

SECOND READING (1 CORINTHIANS 11:23-26)
Every time you eat this bread and drink this cup, you are proclaiming the death of the Lord

It is ironic that liturgical abuses should give rise to the oldest account of the Christian liturgy. Among the many problems of Paul's community in Corinth, charity, unity and good manners were being flouted in the assemblies gathered for the celebration of the Lord's Supper. When Paul counters such conduct, he takes the opportunity of explaining the proper meaning of what they were celebrating. He makes it clear that this explanation comes from tradition, given by the Lord himself.

The memorial of the death of Christ proclaims the abiding presence of Christ's sacrifice for our redemption, and the pledge of our future glory with him. It is the *new* covenant, as foretold by Jeremiah, sealed in blood like the covenant between God and Moses.

There is no new doctrine in this for the Corinthians. From early times, the Church has looked back to the night of the Last Supper to see in the sacramental offering of her Lord the foundation of her most sacred rite.

THIRD READING (JOHN 13:1-15)
Now he showed how perfect his love was

When Jesus' Hour had come his public proclamation was ended. He now turns to the sheep given to him by his Father and instructs them about the glorification his Hour brings.

The example he gives them is not just a lesson in simple humility. The Hour is much too important for that. This sign, too, must be referred to his glorification. The washing of the feet brings out the type of path he must tread to return to his Father, that of humiliation and submission; it stresses that his own must be incorporated in this mystery of humility. Peter has to submit because otherwise he will have 'no part' in Jesus. Even a phrase like 'laying aside his garments' may refer to the laying down of his life. The washing of the feet thus becomes a sign of the Way of the Lord. When the disciples follow the same path of humility, they share in the glorification of the Father that he achieved. It brings them union with Jesus, and the communion of charity with their fellow disciples.

John had no need to repeat what he said about the Bread of Life (in chapter six). The glorified Jesus is still present among his disciples, especially in the sign that proves his unending love, the eucharist.

The theme of sacrificial victim thus pervades this Last Supper memorial. The offering of Christ to his Father becomes his glorification and man's redemption; his blood spilled in death becomes our purification and protection. If it does not remain the sign of love, what else is it? In the words of Paul to the Corinthians : 'What am I to say to you?' if the death of the Lord is profaned among you.

GOOD FRIDAY: THE COMMEMORATION OF THE LORD'S PASSION *27 March 1970*

The Good Friday liturgy can only concern the suffering and humiliation of Christ.

John has told us so often in his Gospel that the work of Jesus is submission to his Father's command by the laying down of his life. The Epistle to the Hebrews so stresses the humanity of Christ, that not even knowledge of the outcome takes away the agony he suffered—he has been tried in every way. It is left to the Suffering Servant Song to show us the torments of his death, and it will not let us forget that our sins have done this.

FIRST READING (ISAIAH 52:13–53:12)
Our faults struck him down in death

Even the sublime theology of the Servant Songs of Isaiah surpasses itself in the Fourth Song. It is set in dialogue form between God and the pagan nations. Though God declares the triumph of his servant at the beginning, the converted Gentile nations and their kings recoil in horror at the condition of the Servant. He grew up among God's own people but was rejected by them. He became one with them to take on their sins. As silent in his sufferings as a lamb, he is condemned and killed. Yet he has been innocent and dedicated to God's service to the very last. Because of his atoning death, God gives him life out of death. The Servant has experienced the sins of many in order to save them; but this has been his glorification.

The Gospels abound with allusions to this Song. Jesus himself saw this figure as the forerunner of his own mission. And the early Church considered her Lord as the Servant's perfect fulfilment.

In death, Jesus commends his spirit to his Father for vindication and glorification. THE RESPONSORIAL PSALM cries for salvation from oppression and thanks God when deliverance comes.

SECOND READING (HEBREWS 4:14-16; 5:7-9)
He learnt to obey through suffering and became for all who obey him the source of eternal salvation

The author has explained that Jesus has been set up as the

94

great high priest, worthy of our full confidence and faith; now according to his plan, he must show how Jesus has been compassionate towards us; how he was fully aware of our temptations and weaknesses. Jesus experienced all these things himself. He feared death because he so embraced the human state; he prayed and suffered silent anguish to be delivered *through* his redemptive death. So through obedient suffering he becomes the perfect sacrifice and priest, and thus is for others the source of all salvation. Because of Jesus, God's throne is now the place we can approach for the benefits we need. He himself intercedes for us continually with his Father.

So close to the theology of this passage is the Hymn of the Epistle to the Philippians set for the Gospel acclamation.

THIRD READING (JOHN 18:1–19:42)
The passion of our Lord Jesus Christ

When we talk of the Passion of our Lord in St John's Gospel, what does this really mean? For, if anything, Jesus is the supreme actor in this drama. More than in the other Gospels, Jesus is in control. In John the crucifixion becomes even more laden with meaning. In John the cross itself assumes all the saving events, as the place and time of Christ's victory, and his Hour of Triumph foreseen and planned by the Father. It is a humiliation, yet exaltation within its humiliation, and the reversal of all such a death should mean. Like its sign in the washing of the feet, it incorporates all into a new world of love and obedience to the Father. From the cross flow the symbols of the Father's love, the Spirit and the Church; water and blood (these also are the signs of baptism and the eucharist). Christ's cross in St John presides over all. As king he *rules* from a tree.

Was the suffering and humiliation necessary? If Jesus was God, wasn't there some other way? We need no reminder of the themes that accompany suffering, we know them all too well. This is perhaps the point in answer to these questions. If God is going to respect us as human beings, then he has to reveal himself and his love for us in ways that we will understand. It is by being personal with us that he does it. Can there be any greater demonstration of love, says our Lord, than the laying down of life itself for a friend?

The liturgy of the Paschal Vigil gives everything that the Church has got, because it tells us all she is. It expresses the simple cry of victory: 'He is risen!'

The long ceremony has as many as nine readings. Not all the Old Testament passages, of which there are seven, are obligatory, nor should they be considered so. However, three should be read, among which the Lectionary demands we place the account of the Crossing of the Red Sea which laid the foundation for God's preparatory covenant. These readings from the Law and the prophets build up the picture of the whole of salvation history before Christ. Whatever choice is made, to explain the texts within the unity of God's plan is paramount.

THE OLD TESTAMENT READINGS : THE GREAT ACTS AND THE GREAT PROMISES OF GOD

1. *God saw all he had made, and indeed it was very good* (Genesis 1:1–2:2)

The account of creation is stylized by the priestly compilers of the five books of the Law. In spite of later human experience they stress the whole goodness of creation, because everything comes from God through his Word. (Note the stress on God's Word which will come up again in Readings 5 and 6.)

2. *The sacrifice of Abraham, our father in faith* (Genesis 22:1-18)

God, in his preparation to redeem man, chose out Abraham and promised him a family which would grow into a great nation. Yet he was commanded to sacrifice his son. The Church, in reading this, is thinking about the Son who was not spared from death. The Father handed over his own Son because of his faithful love. 'Yahweh provides' not only the ram but the redeemer as well. Isaac is so much the type of Christ silently going to death, only to be snatched from its jaws.

96

3. *The sons of Israel went on dry ground right into the sea* (Exodus 14:15–15:1)

Above all, this Night shows the continuity of God's great acts for his people. The core of the Old Testament is centred around the rescuing of the people from Egypt. In a narration of such apparent simplicity, but great complexity—who is the main actor? God, his angel or Moses? The greatest object of Israel's faith and the guarantee of God's power is put before the Christian people. Christians now have a new Exodus, an escape from death and slavery through the waters of baptism—once again the free gift of God's fidelity and love.

4. *With everlasting love, the Lord your redeemer has taken pity on you* (Isaiah 54:5-14)

As we progress from the Law to the prophetic books, it is the everlasting love of God that is accentuated. The creator and redeemer will be the husband of his people. He punished their offences but will have mercy now. He promises an unending love, which will guarantee his covenant as an everlasting one. Even nature will crumble before this love departs.

5. *Come to me, and your soul will live and I will make an everlasting covenant with you* (Isaiah 55:1-11)

The theme of the everlasting covenant again recurs in the most sublime appreciation of God's Word that the Old Testament ever shows. God's word is his power to achieve all he has promised. The image of food and a banquet is used; the covenant sealed with God's Word will be the food of all the people who have need of it.

6. *In the radiance of the Lord, make your way to light* (Baruch 3:9-15. 32–4:4)

God's Word is a word that is wisdom itself. What is wisdom but to understand God's ways and conduct onself accordingly. The way of God is his Law. Wisdom and the Law are like people who walk among God's people to teach them his way.

97

7. *I shall pour clean water over you and you will be cleansed*
(Ezekiel 36:16-28)

The final Old Testament passage comes from Ezekiel and
shows how God punishes his people only to reveal to them his
glory and holiness. His holiness means that he is going to gather
them from among all the nations; wash away their sins; give
them a new heart and a new spirit; renew them; keep them in
his commandments; set them to live in the land of their ancestors.
God's covenant will stand again with its same formula :

'You shall be my people, and I shall be your God.'

Notice, among the RESPONSORIAL PSALMS, the Victory Hymn
after the Third Reading. Many think this is the oldest passage
in the Old Testament, composed after the Exodus itself.

THE NEW TESTAMENT READINGS : THE VICTORY OF CHRIST

1. *Christ having been raised from the dead, will never die again*
(Romans 6:3-11)

In the Easter vigil, this reading from Romans is of crucial
importance as it gathers together the essential themes of the
celebration. The Christian shares in the very act by which Christ
died and rose again. He is freed by his union with Christ from
the state of sin and death which until now has been part of his
innermost being.

Christ is the once-for-all salvation event. He died to that sinful
state of humanity which is the ambit of all that opposes God,
and now lives to God. Our baptism brought us out of the tomb
when we rose to live with Christ. It is up to us to return the love
and fidelity which God shows us. Only a real and genuine freedom from sin is a real and genuine freedom from death.

2. *Jesus of Nazareth, who was crucified, has risen* (Gospel)
(Mark 16:1-8)

After the long Passion narrative, the post-resurrection verses
are brief and somewhat confused. Though the resurrection is the
centre of the Christian mystery it is never described in the New
Testament.

Mark seems to feel a weakness even to give a proper glimpse

of this supreme act of God. His joy and happiness is tempered with unbelieving amazement. He shows that the greatest manifestation of the divine activity leaves the women thunderstruck, so totally unprepared were they for what had happened on that Sunday morning. They are told that Christ is going to set up his community again and lead them to Galilee—the place of their former intimacy. But they are afraid to deliver the message to Peter and the others.

Christ's resurrection is the centre of the dramatic reversal that the Christian message preaches. It is the centre of the history of salvation, the event prepared for and promised by God for thousands of years.

If men go to any person to look for life, could they ask for anything more than to go to Jesus of Nazareth to ask for it? It is so simple, yet we say we need the gift of faith. Yes, faith is required. Nowhere more eloquently than in the Paschal Vigil is the mystery of faith expressed.

EASTER SUNDAY, MORNING MASS   *29 March 1970*

Joy in the risen Christ should pervade this Mass.

The Gospel gives John's account of the Empty Tomb, with all the personal touches of a man who was on scene. (At an evening Mass the moving story of the Appearance to the disciples on the road to Emmaus may replace the day Gospel.) The Epistle to the Colossians may worry about errors, but no Christian will go wrong if he keeps his mind fixed on the risen Christ; nor will abuses of the community at Corinth be tolerated if the paschal mysteries inspire their hearts. Especially in Peter's sermon from the Acts of the Apostles do we feel the joy the disciples felt in the presence of their risen Master—their community was complete again, not with a Jesus doomed to suffer, but with the Lord of the living and the dead.

FIRST READING (ACTS 10:34. 37-43)
We have eaten and drunk with him after his resurrection

So often the Sermons of Acts give syntheses of the early Christian preaching. Luke is usually very careful about his sources. However, he is obviously addressing Christians in general in this passage; they would know about the happenings in Jerusalem more than the 'God-fearers' of Caesarea.

The story given by Peter comes down to the fact that God has chosen special men as *witnesses* of the risen Lord. The Lord lived among them, and this for Peter meant that he has to go out to proclaim it, demanding complete commitment to Jesus now vindicated. This is now the word of life.

The traditional Easter Psalm is used in the RESPONSORIAL PSALM. It is a processional community thanksgiving, praising God for the day he has brought about.

SECOND READING (COLOSSIANS 3:1-4)
You must look for the things that are in heaven, where Christ is

Colossians is so much the Epistle of Christ, head of the Church, his body. Errors are attacked and concern for the elements of this world condemned. Instead of being tied to human regulations, our minds and hearts should be turned heavenwards, because of the victory Christ has already won. He died to the world of human institutions. We are buried with him (in baptism) and

100

look up to heaven (in faith). Christ has only to be revealed in his final glory for everything to be complete.

ALTERNATIVE SECOND READING (1 CORINTHIANS 5:6-8)
Get rid of all the old yeast, and make yourselves into a completely new batch of bread

Paul's community in Corinth is split with rivalries, and a serious case of incest has been discovered in the community. The removal of such an offender from the assembly reminds Paul of the way we should approach our Christianity—with a new broom, a clean sweep, a new yeast. These verses suggest that he composed this Letter about Easter 57 AD.

THIRD READING (JOHN 20:1-9)
He must rise from the dead

The story of the Empty Tomb in John gives one the impression that he is telling how the penny dropped for the disciples. Till now they did not understand. John has told us so often that they did not really *see* things until the Glorification of Jesus. He now stresses vision; they saw the cloths lying there, and the odd position of one of the shrouds. They saw and believed. Now the Spirit could come and show them, because Jesus' Hour had come. It was necessary that he should be glorified so that true belief could come to men. (*Note:* The Gospel of the Paschal Vigil may be used as an alternative at Masses during the day.)

ALTERNATIVE THIRD READING, EVENING MASS (LUKE 24:13-35)
Stay with us; it is nearly evening

The Emmaus story can be read if Mass is celebrated in the evening. It shows the gradual dawning of faith on the disciples on the road. Jesus interpreted the Law and the Prophets for them and showed himself in the breaking of bread. The story may show that in Luke's mind Jesus was especially interested in the missionary traveller.

The Easter Day Mass is one that stresses the presence of the risen Jesus among his own, leading them to the fullness of faith. Easter joy can be expressed so eminently in the words of the two disciples as they prepared to hurry back to Jerusalem : 'Did not our hearts burn within us as he talked to us on the road and explained the scriptures to us?'

101

SECOND SUNDAY OF EASTER   5 *April 1970*

This Sunday, the Octave of Easter, continues the Easter joy by appealing to the faith that forms the Christian community in one heart.

The Gospel gives the story of Jesus' breathing the Spirit onto his disciples, and adds the account of Thomas' doubting and John's purpose in writing his book. First John talks of the relationship of faith and love, while Luke stresses the similar unity of heart and soul that was found in those early days in Jerusalem.

FIRST READING (ACTS 4:32-35)

United, heart and soul

Luke's purpose in Acts is to relate the witness of the early Church as directed by the Holy Spirit. Especially through the great witnesses, Peter and Paul, the word goes out from Jerusalem to the ends of the earth.

Jerusalem saw the springtime of the Church. Three 'progress reports' note the spread of the Way of God and its effect on the people of the Holy City. Today's First Reading gives the second such 'progress report'.

The apostles as chosen witnesses of Christ's resurrection boldly continue the proclamation. But Luke underscores the unity of the faithful, seen especially in the sharing of possessions. To say that Luke is idealizing the situation does not render the communion of goods suspect today. Not all the Christians took part in the pool. It is the unity and love such a gesture expresses that is important for Paschaltide.

The Easter Psalm of thanksgiving is again used.

SECOND READING (1 JOHN 5:1-6)

Anyone who has been begotten of God has already overcome the world

The concatenation of words and phrases in this Reading is quite remarkable even in a letter noted for such things. Holding primacy over the marks of the Christian is his faith, the source of all his blessings. Perhaps it would be better to say, faith is the element which reveals the presence of all the others.

To believe that Jesus is the Son of God
= to have been born of God

102

= to love God
= to love other disciples
= to obey God's commandments
= to overcome the world with victory.

Faith is the victory over the powers of darkness. It allows the characteristics of the child of God to become operative. The blood and water from the cross flow through the Spirit into the hearts of all men of faith, giving them a share in Jesus through baptism and the holy eucharist. In the external sacrament and the internal Spirit, Jesus is the Saviour of the world.

THIRD READING (JOHN 20:19-31)

Eight days later, Jesus came

This Sunday and next Sunday the Gospels continue to relate the appearances of Jesus to his disciples.

In today's Gospel, three separate things are combined.

Firstly, Jesus concludes his Hour of glorification by appearing to his disciples on Easter Sunday evening, and formally imparting to them the Spirit he 'gave up' on the cross. The spiritual qualities of the risen Lord are especially noticed by John. Jesus is received with great joy. His Word bestows the peace that only he can give. The Spirit is now given them for their new divine mission. John demonstrates from our Lord's words that it is the Spirit who is responsible for the Church's power to mediate judgment. This passage is used by Trent to refer to the Sacrament of Penance.

Secondly, the incident a week later, with Thomas, brings the Gospel to its most explicit profession of faith in the Risen Lord— 'My Lord and my God'. This is what Jesus is for the successive generations of Christians, expressed with the solemnity that describes the one true God in the Old Testament.

Thirdly, John can now close his Gospel confident that his purpose has been achieved.

Faith is the beginning of our salvation. This Mass shows it must be a paschal faith, a belief in Jesus as risen Lord. Only faith sealed with baptism makes us children of God and members of Christ. None of the Gospels is more sacramental than John, yet he stresses more vividly than the other evangelists the need for faith. Only when faith comes with utter conviction can the sacrament of God's love, the eucharist, have its full effect, and bring the paschal joy to genuine completion.

Forgiveness of sins is the effect of Christ's victory. Paschaltide remembers this with joy.

The Gospel is Luke's account of the final appearance of Jesus to his disciples, when he gave them their mission to preach throughout the world. The Reading from Acts shows Peter in action, carrying out the Lord's command in word and deed by preaching the forgiveness of sins. The passage from First John remembers the weaknesses of us all, but we are blessed with the intercession of Jesus before his Father.

FIRST READING (ACTS 3:13-15. 17-19)
You killed the prince of life. God however raised him from the dead

When Peter carries out Christ's command to preach in his name, we find in the accounts of Acts not just word of mouth proclamation, but the witness to Jesus in deeds of healing. Peter heals the cripple who sat before the 'Beautiful Gate' of the Temple, and he does it 'in the name of Jesus of Nazareth'.

His sermon then explains the sign he has just performed. It is faith in Jesus that causes the man to be healed.

Already in the sermon the divine names of the Old Testament start being applied to Jesus: the Holy One, the Just One, the Prince of Life. The name 'Servant' is also given to the Lord.

What Luke wants to stress in this sermon is that the missionary proclamation gives no more excuse for ignorance about what was happening. God's plan took consideration of ignorance when Jesus was condemned; but now the issue is clear. Once the resurrection has been achieved, excuses must cease; men who now refuse to be convinced are numbered with the impenitent leaders who put the Lord to death. For those who repent and believe, God will look at their sins no longer.

THE RESPONSORIAL PSALM sings of the wonders and blessings God presents to those he loves.

SECOND READING (1 JOHN 2:1-5)
He is the sacrifice that takes our sins away, and not only ours, but the whole world's

John's subject in this letter is the Word of life—to live this life is to believe in God's Son, and show this in love.

Living in faith is living in the light. What does this mean? We can tell that we live in the light when no sin grips us, when God's commandment of faith, love and submission are in us, when we do not give in to the false standards of this world.

So often John walks on the mountain peaks. He does not compromise the real meaning of the redemption. He means us to live the same kind of life as Christ lives, sinless and utterly committed to God. But even John takes a realistic approach into his vision. We can and do sin; we do tone down the brightness of Christ's light in ourselves. But Jesus, in his love, heals this by his intercession with his Father.

Jesus is called the advocate or paraclete in this Letter. Not until the Gospel does John reserve this title for the Holy Spirit.

THIRD READING (LUKE 24:35-48)
So you see how it is written that the Christ would suffer and on the third day rise from the dead

Last week, John's account of the missionary mandate to the disciples was heard; this Sunday it is Luke's.

Perhaps it is strange that it should be the final appearance of our Lord that dispels the doubts of his apostles. There is a purpose in this. They are witnesses of his resurrection *in order that* they might go out to preach his message. Till this mission is given, says Luke, they are not really witnesses to the resurrection event. Jesus does not show himself to *prove* his resurrection, but to stir up their conviction.

Luke then explains the origin of apostolic witness as the vision of the risen Christ. But this is not all. Jesus opens up the meaning of the scriptures for his chosen witnesses to interpret. They point to him and explain what he has done. In his name, not the Old Testament divine name, they preach the forgiveness of sins, which is none other than the restoration of God's favour.

The mastery over sin that Christ's death brings is, in the mind of St Luke, the message people want to hear. A victory of the magnitude of the resurrection is needed to root out the evils from man's heart. In the Christian, the presence of the Lord should banish the fears brought by evil, and create a Christian optimism. But the foundations will have to shake, so long as the mission of Christ is to continue.

105

FOURTH SUNDAY OF EASTER   *19 April 1970*

This Sunday is devoted to the theme of the Good Shepherd.

The Good Shepherd discourse so much resembles the Last Supper discourses. In talking about his sheep Jesus is talking about his own, given to him by his Father. In First John, they are called God's children, destined for the vision of God as he is. Acts recounts another sermon of Peter on the occasion of the first persecutions for preaching Christ's message.

FIRST READING (ACTS 4:8-12)
This is the only name by which we can be saved

For continuing Jesus' ministry of preaching and healing, the apostles, Peter and John, meet the same fate as their Master. They are arrested, and with that the persecutions of the Church begin right at her birthplace, in Jerusalem.

Peter speaks out boldly, with the voice of God's Spirit, to the leaders of Israel responsible for Christ's death. The Sadducees would not accept any resurrection. Both they and the other Sanhedrin members stood by the Old Testament prerogatives of God. Yet here Peter tears it all down. Only in the name of the Jesus they executed is salvation to be gained—and he has risen to prove it!

We have experienced the humiliation of Christ in the weeks of Lent; Paschaltide sees the reversal of this, by God's preordained plan. Jesus triumphs over his enemies, but also becomes the keystone to a new building, his Church.

The persecution of the apostles will result in the dispersal of Christians from Jerusalem and the call of the Gentiles.

THE RESPONSORIAL PSALM makes use of the paschal psalm of thanksgiving.

SECOND READING (1 JOHN 3:1-2)
We shall see God as he really is

John has already described in this Letter the conditions for living in the light of Christ. The verses of this Reading change his subject. Now he wants to consider living as children of God.

God's gift to us has been his Son. In this Son it becomes possible for us to become God's sons. We are already the children of God, begotten of him through our faith. God's love has done this for us, but even now prepares for greater joys. We know God only in faith. When the time comes, the image through faith will give way to the intimacy and immediacy of seeing God face to face, of loving him as he loves us. This is his ultimate gift in his Son.

THIRD READING (JOHN 10:11-18)
The good shepherd is one who lays down his life for his sheep

The Paschaltide liturgy has long used the discourse on the good shepherd to typify the relationship between Jesus and his disciples. It is not a discourse of sentimentality, but of life and death struggles and divine mystery.

King David once protected his flock at the risk of his own life. And always in the Old Testament the theme of the shepherd was associated with kingship and power. The shepherd of Israel was her king. So Jesus is the true and perfect shepherd of Israel.

This means that God's people belong to Jesus, and not only the people of Israel, but those outside the fold, the gentile sheep.

But how is Jesus' government exercised? By obeying his Father's command to die for his sheep. They become completely his, because he gives up everything for them, deliberately and knowingly. This is the way set by his Father's love.

There are so many paradoxes of logic here. For John, as always, Jesus becomes the good shepherd at the Hour of laying down his life. At that moment when his Spirit is given up, his sheep become really his. Hence the good shepherd discourse is a paschal Gospel. We are his sheep because that Hour has come.

The liturgy today speaks of what Christ has made us in his paschal mystery. More expressive even than the shepherd-king relationship with his sheep, is the closeness of union as brothers with the same Father. Christ is our king and judge, but in faith he is more our friend and companion. This idea is a strong one, as powerful as is any great friendship. He stands glorified in his Hour as the support of all his faithful.

FIFTH SUNDAY OF EASTER   *26 April 1970*

Paschaltide brings out the theme of union with Christ. This is seen especially in today's Gospel.

The Church's mission to the world was largely opened up by Paul; the First Reading recalls his early days as a follower of Christ. In the continuing readings from First John, obedience to the commandment of faith and love points out the true child of God. The Gospel reads one of the favourite passages from the Fourth Gospel—'I am the true vine'.

FIRST READING (ACTS 9:26-31)
Barnabas explained how the Lord had appeared to Saul on his journey

It is hard to imagine either the New Testament or the early Church without the figure of Paul. Yet he himself and the words of the Acts of the Apostles (on several occasions) tell us that Paul was not always a Christian; in fact he persecuted the Church of God.

Already when Paul is converted, Luke's plan in Acts is well developed. The Gospel has spread into Judaea and Samaria. Paul's conversion introduces a pause in the book, before Peter launches that mission to the Gentile nations which Paul will bring to completion.

It is important that Barnabas explains to the apostles in Jerusalem Paul's credentials. Paul has seen the risen Christ as Lord; this vision was a witness-appearance, just as the appearances of the Lord to the apostles ordained them for the same witness. The sight of the Lord makes Paul as fearless as Stephen, at whose death he had assisted. Paul fell under the spell of the risen Christ; a joyful and irresistible spirit was given him to proclaim Jesus to the ends of the earth.

THE RESPONSORIAL PSALM sings of the blessing God gives after deliverance from evils and distress. This psalm is a traditional one for Holy Week.

SECOND READING (1 JOHN 3:18-24)
His commandments are these: that we believe in his Son and that we love one another

The conditions for being God's child are, for John, similar to those for living in the light. We have to refrain from sin, remain

108

unattached to the world and false doctrines, and keep God's commandments.

One is never quite sure how many commandments there are in John. God demands submission, faith, love, humility etc. Does John leave us any means of telling which is the most important? He does, but not quite in the way we think. We need to hold fast to the centrality of faith in John's thoughts, especially in a Letter where the love-commandment is in such high relief.

To talk of commandments is really to look at one commandment from various points of view. *The* commandment is to believe in Jesus as God's Son. But it also shows itself in love, since the test of faith is our devotion to God's service. But *the real test* of believing and loving is how we love and respect our fellow disciples in Christ. (Not all men, notice, though this may be implicit.) Only when this test is positive can we really say we carry out God's commandments and live as his children.

THIRD READING (JOHN 15:1-8)
Whoever remains in me, with me in him, bears fruit in plenty

This passage is John's equivalent to Paul's doctrine on the mystical body of Christ. Jesus speaks to his own as if he is already glorified. We know that so many parts of this Gospel presuppose the Hour of Jesus. This is especially true when Jesus presents himself with the words 'I am . . .', as in 'I am the bread of life', 'I am the resurrection and the life'.

When Jesus says 'I am the true vine', he could not forget that the vine of the Old Testament is Israel herself. In these words, he takes on himself the whole of his people, and forms them anew with his own glorified life. His disciples receive this life, thus beginning the new community of God.

In using this image, our Lord speaks directly to his disciples who continue his mission in bearing fruit. They possess his message of revelation by remaining in him. But he does not exclude from bearing fruit those not given hierarchical mission. To bear fruit is the privilege and task of all who share Jesus' life.

The life of Jesus has been poured into men through the resurrection. It can bear fruit in the missionary zeal of a man like Paul. It can fossilize in a person's heart. But there always remains the test for genuineness. Does it bear fruits of faith, love and humility in others? If not, it may not really be Christ's life at all.

Paschal joy is authentic joy because it is rooted in love. There is a commandment to love because God himself is love. These are the themes of this Mass.

The commandment of the new covenant can be seen to be the Christian duty to love. In the Gospel, Jesus asks for its fulfilment, if his disciples are going to remain rooted in him. First John gives unparalleled expression to what God is really like, by describing him as Love. To remind us that Pentecost approaches, the reading from Acts gives the account of the 'Pentecost of the Gentiles'.

FIRST READING (ACTS 10:25-26. 34-35. 44-48)

The gift of the Holy Spirit has been poured out on the pagans too

Under the auspices of the apostle Peter, the Church enters a new stage in her mission by preaching to the pagans. It begins modestly enough, however, in the household of Cornelius of Caesarea.

It is hard to envisage the position of the early Church with regard to non-Jews. For Jews, trafficking with pagans in any sort of way was sacrilege. But Luke sees the Spirit directing this venture of Peter. (Peter's sermon was used in the Mass of Easter Sunday, so it is omitted here to allow the Reading to get to the main point.) The Holy Spirit forces Peter's hand by coming down on those listening to him, with the same effects as were felt by the apostles in the 'Pentecost of the Jews' (Acts 2). Baptism of water only sets the seal on 'baptism' of the Spirit, but it is made in the name of Jesus the risen Lord, whom Peter has just proclaimed.

THE RESPONSORIAL PSALM is a hymn in praise of the salvation of God, which reaches out to the nations of the earth.

SECOND READING (1 JOHN 4:7-10)

God is love

In the first part of John's Letter, he has often discussed faith and love. Now he compares them, firstly talking about love, as in this present Reading, and then about faith.

What our redemption is all about, and indeed what God is all about can be summed up in one word—love.

It is not, in John's mind, love in any neutral sense. We have to see it in action to know what it is. We do have such an action to judge by: God sent his only Son because of his love for us. This love, then, means giving up what is most dear, or thinking about others more than overselves, or feeling that nothing is too much trouble. But all this put on a divine plane! That God acts for love and is himself love means there is no worldly definition for it. We believe what it is; and we describe it by recounting the message of our salvation.

THIRD READING (JOHN 15:9-17)
A man can have no greater love than to lay down his life for his friends

This Sunday's Gospel continues the chapter in the Last Supper Discourse dedicated to the true vine. Now, remaining in Jesus is seen as remaining in his love.

Jesus has made it plain that the whole of our salvation comes from the divine initiative. The Father's love planned it all. In fact the relationship of Father and Son is contained within an ambit of love. Father's command and Son's humble submission are all for love.

If we can get any meaning from this mystery it comes from the understanding that the fulfilling of the commandment of love will bring us into the divine circle of love. It will not make it humanly easier for us, since dying for someone could hardly be easy. But it gives us a new life, a new vision, a joy that human success can never match.

For the disciples this entering of the divine ambit of love is going to demand the fulfilment of the commission to bear God's revelation to others, so that these too can enter into the fullness of divine love.

A few condensed theological remarks like these always seem mere words. The liturgy today harnesses the deepest theological mysteries before the 'departure' of the Lord at his Ascension. It is no censure on the difficulty of these readings to note that the Readings of the Seventh Sunday of Easter may replace the ones of this Mass, if the Ascension is put off until Sunday next.

THE FEAST OF THE ASCENSION 7 *May 1970*

This feast celebrates a twofold mystery, the ascension of Jesus to his Father and his enthronement at his Father's right hand. It was not always a separate feast. Largely influenced by the words of Acts 1:3, the feast of our Lord's enthronement was introduced in the fourth century.

The Gospel uses Mark's version of the Lord's command to go out and preach, concluded by the ascension account. The Epistle to the Ephesians tells of the power of God to work in the resurrection and exaltation of Christ. The First Reading is dedicated to the fullest ascension account, that of Acts.

FIRST READING (ACTS 1:1-11)
He was lifted up while they looked on

The verses of the ascension story form the prologue to the book of Acts, a sequel to the Gospel of Luke. They are highly theological, which can cause confusion if a rigid historical accuracy is demanded.

Luke states his plan and purpose for the Acts, by the interplay of two of his basic theological themes (the Holy Spirit and Jerusalem) with the geographical structure of the book—*from* Jerusalem *throughout* Judaea and Samaria *to* the ends of the earth. The Holy Spirit is to guide the Church on a world-wide expansion programme, but first the disciples have to await his coming. They are thus in an interim period between the resurrection of Jesus and the sending of the Spirit. The forty days could be symbolic for this period of waiting. When Jesus is enthroned in heaven, then will the Spirit be sent.

A Royal Psalm is used in the RESPONSORIAL PSALM to praise the universal dominion of God.

SECOND READING (EPHESIANS 1:17-23)
He made him sit at his right hand in heaven

Paul thanks God for the faith of his Ephesian converts and at the same time prays that God will give them the spiritual insight into the mystery of the divine purpose. God is going to bring all men into one single unity with Christ as its head; the dividing wall of Jew and pagan will be broken down.

The gift needed to appreciate this great work of God is the same sort of perception that is required to experience the power of God which lifted Christ up from the dead and brought him to exaltation in heaven. The same power that achieved in one event, resurrection, ascension and exaltation, in the same event incorporates the Church (and her members) into a heavenly existence.

In Paul's terms, the Church celebrates today her Lord's enthronement with his Father. But she also commemorates her own entry into that same heavenly sanctuary with the Head from whom she draws her existence. The Church gains her privileges from the enthroned Lord.

THIRD READING (MARK 16:15-20)
He was taken up into heaven; there at the right hand of God he took his place

For Mark, as well as for Matthew and Luke, the final appearance of Jesus to his disciples was when he gave them their mission to preach. Even at this late hour he discovered their reluctance to believe.

The disciples are to preach the Good News: for those who believe, it will be for their salvation; for those who reject their word, it will result in condemnation by God. They will be able to work signs to show the power of God's kingdom at work in their message.

When Mark talks about the Lord's departure, he expresses it in two stages, the ascension and the exaltation to God's right hand. But Jesus still worked among his chosen messengers to communicate his revelation to the whole world.

The Readings indicate, then, a duality of themes; Jesus ascends to his Father, where he is exalted to his deserved place at the Father's right hand. Though we can say with truth that the work of Christ was complete on Easter Sunday, even the New Testament starts the trend to celebrate the different aspects of the Paschal Mystery over many weeks. The feast of the Ascension was the last one to be introduced into the Paschal Cycle, but it does help to underscore the acceptance of Christ's sacrifice and his continuing intercession for us at his Father's side. The great result of that intercession is the sending of the Holy Spirit.

113

SEVENTH SUNDAY OF PASCHALTIDE   *10 May 1970*

The themes of unity and love predominate in this Mass, in anticipation of the founding of the Church at Pentecost.

In the Priestly Prayer, Christ remembers especially the ministry of his disciples for the unification of mankind. The final Reading from First John continues the love theme. And in the Acts of the Apostles, the College of Twelve is completed by the election of Matthias.

FIRST READING (ACTS 1:15-17. 20-26)

We must therefore choose out one of these to be a witness to his resurrection with us

In the Gospels, our Lord seemed to have especially desired to have a group of twelve men to form the nucleus of his new community, on the model of the twelve tribes of Israel. This will go a long way in helping to see why Peter should be so anxious to replace Judas and restore the number of twelve.

But it is likely that Luke himself considered it important to stress this story. The one hundred and twenty persons waiting in the upper room were to be endowed with the Holy Spirit. They could then begin their mission as stipulated by the Lord. For this work they would need the correct number of officers, that is, twelve. So Peter, for the rest, suggested they make up this number.

In this passage, however, Luke seems very anxious to give us the criterion for membership of this group of Twelve, which he, more than any other of the New Testament authors, terms apostles, and is followed in this by the tradition of the Church. To secure the absolute authenticity of the Church about to be formed, that early group had to have as their leaders those men who (i) had been with Jesus from the very beginning of his public life, and (ii) had seen the risen Lord and been appointed witness of his resurrection.

THE RESPONSORIAL PSALM praises the greatness of a God who loves all those who show him reverence, and takes away their sins.

SECOND READING (1 JOHN 4:11-16)

Anyone who lives in love lives in God, and God lives in him

The final reading from this Epistle of the Love of God takes

114

us into the heart of the Trinity itself. To live the life of faith means that the Son has really saved us; to live the life of love means that we have a share in God's Spirit. It is true that we have not seen God, but the communication of life in faith and love that he has given us, has already let us into the secret, that the essence of God is to be found in the love that has made him do such things for us. The love that is God banishes fear, hatred and rivalry.

In this Letter we live in a new world where God is the only one who catches the writer's eye; he, like us, can only find God in the man Jesus, whom he believes makes God known as only God's Son can.

THIRD READING (JOHN 17:11-19)
May they be one like us!

As the eucharistic prayer in the Mass consecrates the offerings, so the priestly prayer of Jesus tells the whole meaning of his life and consecrates him for the sacrifice of his Hour. It is also the prayer for the consecration of Jesus' disciples in their mission to men, and for the Church they form.

In the verses of this Gospel Reading, it is the relationship of Jesus to his disciples that is paramount. Jesus prays to his 'Holy Father', asking that his Father's holiness will keep his disciples faithful to their discipleship, by keeping them sanctified from the world. They have chosen to take the road of discipleship, received the word of revelation and accepted the apostolic mission. Now the Father must keep them true to the divine sphere they have entered, though they still remain in the world to carry on his work.

Jesus' act of consecration is also his supreme act of revealing himself. So he asks his Father that the disciples too may share in the consecration to the supreme message of salvation—Jesus Son of God and Lord of all.

Paschaltide thus brings about the joy of belonging to God, of being a child of God, of being loved by God. It brings us into the heart of the Paschal Mystery. Having told us on Easter Sunday to look for the things that are in heaven, the liturgy practises what she preaches. She has gone heavenwards, on the wings of the Apostle John.

115

The theme of this Vigil Mass of Pentecost is the expectation of the Holy Spirit. The Mass may be celebrated at some time during the evening of the Vigil. The Gospel gives the note of expectancy, 'there was no Spirit as yet', and this is shared by the text of Romans which talks about the Spirit of Hope.

FIRST READING

Two texts from the Law and two from the Prophets are offered for the First Reading. Only one need be read.

1. *It was named Babel because there the language of the whole earth was confused* (Genesis 11:1-8)

The story of the Tower of Babel forms a climax to the primitive history of man as told by Genesis. The Tower incident caused the complete disunity between man and man, as well as between man and God. The city (called 'Gate of God') and its ziggurat tower became symbols of the revolt against God. The call of the patriarchs will begin the reversal of disunity, a process that will be completed at Pentecost.

2. *The Lord came down on the mountain of Sinai before all the people* (Exodus 19:3-8a. 16-20b)

In later Jewish tradition, the Feast of Weeks or Pentecost commemorated the giving of the covenant on Sinai. This reading recalls the greatest blessing of God in the Old Testament, the rescue of his people from Egypt, and the covenant that God was to form with them. He is going to consecrate his people to himself. At Pentecost, the new covenant is ratified and the Paschal Mysteries are completed with the pledge of that covenant, the Holy Spirit.

3. *Dry bones, I am going to make the breath enter you and you will live* (Ezekiel 37:1-14)

This vision is symbolic of the mission of the prophet Ezekiel. He had become the watchman of Israel trying to instil a new spirit into the despondency of the Babylonian exiles. The dry bones were in the valley where he had seen the Glory of God. At Pentecost, the Spirit of God is breathed into those dead from their sins and raises them to life again.

116

4. *Even on the slaves, men and women, will I pour out my spirit* (Joel 3:1-5)

Moses hoped that the spirit of God would come upon all the people. This will now come to pass, says Joel, for the whole nation, from greatest to least will receive the spirit, as if it were a new creation. And signs of a new Exodus will begin God's eternal day. Peter declared this prophecy had come to pass, in his Pentecost sermon (Acts 2).

THE RESPONSORIAL PSALM is traditionally associated with Pentecost. It sings of God's spirit renewing the earth.

SECOND READING (ROMANS 8:22-27)
The Spirit himself expresses our plea in a way that could never be put into words

In this eighth chapter of the Epistle to the Romans, Paul talks about life in the Spirit. God's love has poured into our hearts a new principle of life which is none other than the Holy Spirit.

Paul looks around and finds all the world in eager expectation of receiving a share in the Spirit. All creation shares the lot of man ; as it shared his misery, so it will share his glory. We wait in hope for that future glory; creation waits with us. The Spirit we possess is only the first-fruits, the pledge of the completion of our salvation. The Spirit is so intimate with God, though, that he can make up for our deficiencies in desires and prayers by pleading with God for what we really need.

At Pentecost, the same Spirit founds in the Church that same hope for the final victory of Christ that the Paschal Mystery has begun to proclaim.

THIRD READING (JOHN 7:37-39)
From his breast shall flow fountains of living water

Of old the prophets looked to Jerusalem to irrigate the earth with her waters. At the Feast of the Tabernacles water was carried in procession to the Temple. It was at the end of such a feast that Jesus called to himself those who would drink at the fountains of life.

But 'there was no Spirit as yet', says the Gospel. The liturgy herself on this Vigil keeps us in suspense until the Day of Pentecost comes around.

The Spirit in the Church is so vividly the theme of this day, when we commemorate the giving of the Spirit to the apostles at the first Pentecost, and the birth of the Church on the same day.

Now the Hour of Jesus has come the Gospel can have no hesitation about telling the story of Jesus breathing out that Spirit on his disciples. Paul can talk about the oneness of the Spirit and the variety of gifts he pours into the Church. As on the Ascension, we have to turn to the pages of Acts to read the account of the descent of the Spirit upon the new people of God.

FIRST READING (ACTS 2:1-11)
They were all filled with the Holy Spirit and began to speak

Only this text of Acts records the events of Pentecost, since the Gospels see the giving of the Spirit in a different light.

In the mind of St Luke this Descent of the Spirit was not just an event but an era. The Old Testament has looked forward to the day when the Spirit would be poured out on all flesh. Now this has come true, the Spirit has the force to recreate the world with the Word of Christ. Luke's Acts is going to show how this is achieved through the mission of the Church to the ends of the earth.

In fire, God came down on Sinai to give the Words of the covenant to Moses. Here is the fire of the new manifestation of God with a new covenant.

The disciples speak with different tongues that all can understand. The Tower of Babel has finished; the disunited human race are now brought together in one tongue by the Spirit of God.

The ecstasies of joys that follow Pentecost complete the joys of Paschaltide.

THE RESPONSORIAL PSALM repeats the traditional Pentecost one sung at the Vigil.

SECOND READING (1 CORINTHIANS 12:3-7. 12-13)
In the one spirit we were all baptized

Among the many troubles Paul had with his converts at Corinth was confusion over the gifts of the Spirit. There seems every indication that the Corinthians were specially endowed with the more spectacular spiritual gifts.

Paul wants them to make a simple test themselves : if anyone refuses to profess the authentic faith then the Spirit of God is not with him. The Spirit first and foremost inspires the correct faith in the Christian.

Many other gifts are distributed by the Holy Spirit, but always for the service of the Church. Not all of them are very extraordinary, but they are nevertheless gifts of the Spirit.

The Spirit is for the Body of Christ. This is where Paul insists the Holy Spirit's role is most prominent. He has returned to the subject of faith, but combined it with the theme of service to the Church. The Spirit is that soul of unity in the Body of Christ that welds together the different nations and classes into the living unity of the people of God.

THIRD READING (JOHN 20:19-23)
As the Father sent me, so I am sending you: receive the Holy Spirit

It is fitting that the Gospel of John should close the Paschaltide cycle of readings, because so often John expresses with the greatest depth what the Church is thinking.

Lord, Spirit and Church are the themes that pervade these four verses :

Lord: Jesus is now glorified, for ever present in his glorified state to all his brethren. He has risen with a spiritual body that will perpetuate the acts of our salvation.

Spirit: The Holy Spirit is given up by Jesus in his Hour, and on Easter evening breathed on his disciples to impart to them the mission to continue his work. They celebrate the sacraments with this Spirit within them. They ponder on their faith with this Spirit to strengthen them.

Church: Jesus sets up his community of disciples with the breathing out of the Spirit, as a people of love, joy and peace. The peace of Christ is in the world because his community is in the world. That peace as the essence of Old and New Testament Blessings is embodied in the gatherings of human beings that embrace it. Peace means that the commandment of fraternal love is being met. The disciples are sent out to carry the peace of the resurrection to all men—the peace between God and man that comes with the outpouring of the Holy Spirit.

Index of Sunday Readings
by the day

Season of Advent

1st Sunday	Isaiah 63:16-17; 64:1. 3-8
	1 Corinthians 1:3-9
	Mark 13:33-37
2nd Sunday	Isaiah 40:1-5. 9-11
	2 Peter 3:8-14
	Mark 1:1-8
3rd Sunday	Isaiah 61:1-2. 10-11
	1 Thessalonians 5:16-24
	John 1:6-8. 19-28
4th Sunday	2 Samuel 7:1-5. 8-11. 16
	Romans 16:25-27
	Luke 1:26-38

Season of Christmas

Christmas:	
Midnight Mass	Isaiah 9:1-7
	Titus 2:11-14
	Luke 2:1-14
Dawn Mass	Isaiah 62:11-12
	Titus 3:4-7
	Luke 2:15-20
Day Mass	Isaiah 52:7-10
	Hebrews 1:1-6
	John 1:1-18
Feast of the Holy Family	Ecclesiasticus 3:2-6. 12-14
	Colossians 3:12-21
	Luke 2:22-40
January. Mary Mother of God	Numbers 6:22-27
	Galatians 4:4-7
	Luke 2:16-21
after Christmas	Ecclesiasticus 24:1-2. 8-12
	Ephesians 1:3-6. 15-18
	John 1:1-18
piphany	Isaiah 60:1-6
	Ephesians 3:2-3. 5-6
	Matthew 2:1-12

Baptism of our Lord	Isaiah 42:1-4. 6-7
	Acts 10:34-38
	Mark 1:7-11

Sundays of the Year

2nd (18 January)	1 Samuel 3:3-10. 19
	1 Corinthians 6:13-15. 17-20
	John 1:35-42
3rd (25 January)	Jonah 3:1-5. 10
	1 Corinthians 7:29-31
	Mark 1:14-20
4th (1 February)	Deuteronomy 18:15-20
	1 Corinthians 7:32-35
	Mark 1:21-28
5th (8 February)	Job 7:1-4. 6-7
	1 Corinthians 9:16-19. 22-23
	Mark 1:29-39

Sundays of Lent

1st	Genesis 9:8-15
	1 Peter 3:18-22
	Mark 1:12-15
2nd	Genesis 22:1-2. 9-13. 15-18
	Romans 8:31-34
	Mark 9:2-10
3rd	Exodus 20:1-17
	1 Corinthians 1:22-25
	John 2:13-25
4th	2 Chronicles 36:14-16. 19-23
	Ephesians 2:4-10
	John 3:14-21
5th	Jeremiah 31:31-34
	Hebrews 5:7-9
	John 12:20-33
Passion Sunday	Mark 11:1-10 (procession)
	Isaiah 50:4-7
	Philippians 2;6-11
	Mark 14:1—15:47
Holy Thursday: Chrism	Isaiah 61:1-3. 6. 8-9
	Apocalypse 1:5-8
	Luke 4:16-21
: Mass of the Lord's Supper	Exodus 12:1-8. 11-14
	1 Corinthians 11:23-26
	John 13:1-15
Good Friday	Isaiah 52:13—53:12
	Hebrews 4:14-16; 5:7-9
	John 18:1—19:42
Easter Vigil	Genesis 1:1—2:2
	Genesis 22:1-18
	Exodus 14:15—15:1
	Isaiah 54:5-14
	Isaiah 55:1-11
	Baruch 3:9-15. 32—4:4
	Ezekiel 36:16-28

121

Mass of Easter Night	Romans 6:3-11
	Mark 16:1-8
Easter Sunday: Morning	Acts 10:34. 37-43
	Colossians 3:1-4
	John 20:1-9
2nd Sunday of Easter	Acts 4:32-35
	1 John 5:1-6
	John 20:19-31
3rd Sunday of Easter	Acts 3:13-15. 17-19
	1 John 2:1-5
	Luke 24:35-48
4th Sunday of Easter	Acts 4:8-12
	1 John 3:1-2
	John 10:11-18
5th Sunday of Easter	Acts 9:26-31
	1 John 3:18-24
	John 15:1-8
6th Sunday of Easter	Acts 10:25-26. 34-35. 44-48
	1 John 4:7-10
	John 15:9-17
Ascension	Acts 1:1-11
	Ephesians 1:17-23
	Mark 16:15-20
7th Sunday of Easter	Acts 1:15-17. 20-26
	1 John 4:11-16
	John 17:11-19
Pentecost	Acts 2:1-11
	1 Corinthians 12:3-7. 12-13
	John 20:19-23

THEMES OF THE SUNDAYS OF LENT

	Old Testament 'Covenant Theme'	Epistle	Gospel
1st Sunday	Noah	Passing through water	Temptation
2nd Sunday	Abraham	God gave his Son for us	Transfiguration
3rd Sunday	Moses	The cross of Christ	Samaritan Woman or Cleansing of the Temple
4th Sunday	Exile and Restoration	Free gift of salvation	Man born blind or Nicodemus
5th Sunday	Promise of new covenant	Jesus our High Priest	Raising of Lazarus or The grain of wheat

122

Index of Scripture References

GENESIS
1:1—2:2   E. Vigil
9:8-15   1 Lent
22:1-2. 9-13. 15-18   2 Lent
22:1-18   E. Vigil

EXODUS
12:1-8. 11-14   H. Thursday
14:15—15:1   E. Vigil
20:1-17   3 Lent

NUMBERS
6:22-27   1 January

DEUTERONOMY
18:15-20   4 Sunday of Year

2 SAMUEL
7:1-5. 8-11. 16   4 Advent

2 CHRONICLES
36:14-16. 19-23   4 Lent

JOB
7:1-4. 6-7   5 Sunday of Year

ECCLESIASTICUS
3:2-6. 12-14   H. Family
24:1-2. 8-12   2 Christmas

ISAIAH
9:1-7   Chr'mas M'night
40:1-5. 9-11   2 Advent
42:1-4. 6-7   Bapt. of O. Lord
50:4-7   Passion
52:7-10   Chr'mas Day
52:3—53:12   G. Friday
54:5-14   E. Vigil
55:1-11   E. Vigil
60:1-6   Epiphany
61:1-2. 10-11   3 Advent

61:1-3. 6. 8-9   H. Thursday
62:11-12   Chr'mas Dawn
63:16-17. 64:1. 3-8   1 Advent

JEREMIAH
31:31-34   5 Lent

EZEKIEL
36:16-28   E. Vigil

JONAH
3:1-5. 10   3 Sunday of Year

BARUCH
3:9-15. 32—4:4   E. Vigil

MATTHEW
2:1-12   Epiphany

MARK
1:1-8   2 Advent
1:7-11   Bapt. of O. Lord
1:12-15   1 Lent
1:14-20   3 Sunday of Year
1:21-28   4 Sunday of Year
1:29-39   5 Sunday of Year
9:2-10   2 Lent
11:1-10   Passion
13:33-37   1 Advent
14:1—15:47   Passion
16:1-8   Easter Night
16:15-20   Ascension

LUKE
1:26-38   4 Advent
2:1-14   Chr'mas M'night
2:15-20   Chr'mas Dawn
2:22-40   Holy Family
2:16-21   1 January
4:16-21   H. Thursday
24:35-48   3 Easter

JOHN
1:1-18   Chr'mas Day
         2 Chr'mas
1:6-8. 19-28   3 Advent
1:35-42   2 Sunday of Year
2:13-25   3 Lent
3:14-21   4 Lent
10:11-18   4 Easter
12:20-33   5 Lent
13:1-15   H. Thursday
15:1-8   5 Easter
15:9-17   6 Easter
17:11-19   7 Easter
18:1—19:42   G. Friday
20:1-9   E. Sunday
20:19-23   Pentecost
20:19-31   2 Easter

ACTS
1:1-11   Ascension
1:15-17. 20-26   7 Easter
2:1-11   Pentecost
3:13-15, 17-19   3 Easter
4:8-12   4 Easter
4:32-35   2 Easter
9:26-31   5 Easter
10:25-26. 34-35. 44-48   6 Easter
10:34-38   Bapt. of O. Lord
10:34. 37-43   E. Sunday

ROMANS
6:3-11   Easter Night
8:31-34   2 Lent
16:25-27   4 Advent

1 CORINTHIANS
1:3-9   1 Advent
1:22-25   3 Lent
6:13-15. 17-20   2 Sunday of Year
7:29-31   3 Sunday of Year
7:32-35   4 Sunday of Year
9:16-19. 22-23   5 Sunday of Year
11:23-26   H. Thursday
12:3-7. 12-13   Pentecost

GALATIANS
4:4-7   1 January

EPHESIANS
1:3-6. 15-18   2 Chr'mas
1:17-23   Ascension
2:4-10   4 Lent
3:2-3. 5-6   Epiphany

PHILIPPIANS
2:6-11   Passion

COLOSSIANS
3:1-4   Easter Sunday
3:12-21   Holy Family

1 THESSALONIANS
5:16-24   3 Advent

HEBREWS
1:1-6   Chr'mas Day
4:14-16; 5:7-9   G. Friday
5:7-9   5 Lent

TITUS
2:11-14   Chr'mas M'night
3:4-7   Chr'mas Dawn

1 PETER
3:18-22   1 Lent

2 PETER
3:8-14   2 Advent

1 JOHN
2:1-5   3 Easter
3:1-2   4 Easter
3:18-24   5 Easter
4:7-10   6 Easter
4:11-16   7 Easter
5:1-6   2 Easter

APOCALYPSE
1:5-8   H. Thursday